MW01289216

The Rise of the Inquisition

AN INTRODUCTION TO THE SPANISH
AND PORTUGUESE INQUISITIONS

Juan Marcos Bejarano Gutierrez

Yaron Publishing
Grand Prairie, Texas

Juan Marcos Bejarano Gutierrez.
Yaron Publishing
701 Forest Park Place
Grand Prairie, Texas 75052
Printed by CreateSpace
www.createspace.com

Book Layout ©2017 BookDesignTemplates.com

Ordering Information:
Quantity sales. Special discounts are available on quantity purchases by corporations, associations, and others. For details, contact the "Special Sales Department" at the address above.

The Rise of the Inquisition / Juan Marcos Bejarano Gutierrez. —1st ed.
ISBN 978-1547222872

Contents

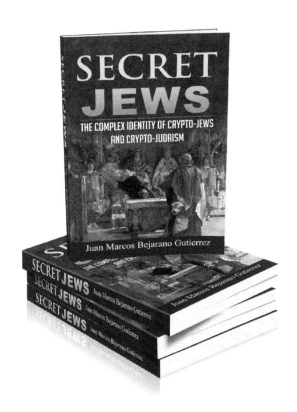

Sign up at CryptoJewishEducation.com
and
Receive the First Chapter of *Secret Jews* Free!

To my sons Eliel Nathan and Yaron Eliav

May they be like Menasseh and Ephraim

"They are martyred so much that in the poverty and abandon to which they were driven by this monster, they kill their own children, burn their husbands, deprive their brothers of life, increase the number of orphans and widows, impoverish the rich, destroy the powerful, make thieves of the nobly born, and sow base and infamous places with modest and chaste women."

—Regarding the Victims of the Inquisition
Samuel Usque
The Consolations for the Tribulations of Israel Translated by Martin Cohen

Introduction

The Inquisition typically conjures up images of intolerance, persecution, and violence and rightly so. Many people think of it as a reflection of the spiritual, scholastic, and scientific darkness of the medieval period. Hundreds of thousands of trials were processed during its lengthy reign. Thousands died at its hand. It seems hard to believe that the Inquisition ended as recently as the third decade of the nineteenth century and then only with some reservations.

The Spanish and Portuguese Inquisitions that began in the late 15th and 16th centuries and lasted well into the 19th century were rooted in the papal inquisitions of the earlier medieval period. The purpose of these tribunals was to arrest and punish persons who deviated from accepted beliefs and practices of the Church. These courts, in turn, were ultimately linked to the religious panels established as early as the reigns of the Roman Emperors Theodosius in the West and Justinian in the East.

The institution as it is now known, began in the thirteenth century when it was set up to combat the heretical sect of the Albigenses. The Albigenses or Cathars embraced Gnostic beliefs that held the God of the New Testament was distinct from the God of the Old Testament. One was opposed to the other.[1] A

---

[1] In 385 CE, the Christian Emperor Maximus tortured and executed the heretic Priscillian and some of his followers. Cecil Roth, *The Spanish Inquisition* (New York: W.W. Norton and Company, 1964), 35. See also Jean Plaidy, *The Spanish Inquisition: Its Rise, Growth, and End* (New York: Barnes and Nobles, 1994), 18. The Inquisition

military crusade was launched against the Albigenses, but the movement went underground. Out of concern for this group, the tribunal was established in several cities in southern France.[2]

The Papacy entrusted the Inquisition to the mendicant orders of Dominicans and Franciscan friars. The mendicant orders were bound by a vow of poverty and an ascetic lifestyle. Local bishops had the authority to investigate heresy, but the mendicant orders provided a more extensive organization. The medieval Inquisition had the power to punish Jews who aided Jewish converts to return to Judaism. The Inquisition also had the authority to order testimony by Jews against lapsed converts. In its early years, however, little attention was paid to Jews other than an occasional action focused on banning or burning certain Jewish books which had been deemed heretical or offensive to Christianity.[3]

---

also targeted Waldesians. The beliefs of the Waldesians are difficult to ascertain but appear to have reflected elements of later Protestant reformers. Joseph Perez, *The Spanish Inquisition: A History* (London: Profile Books, 2006), 101.

[2] The threat of the Albigensian sect was met by severe Inquisitional scrutiny as the historian Cecil Roth noted: "The heresy was apparently stamped out by the so-called Albigensian Crusades from 1209 to 1244, but no sooner had these wars ended in victory for the orthodox party than a fresh problem presented itself. It was discovered that the detested heresy had not been eradicated, but only driven underground, and the idea was conceived that in order to detect and convict heretics it was necessary to employ persons specially qualified for the purpose." Cecil Roth, *The Spanish Inquisition* (New York: W.W. Norton and Company, 1964), 36.

[3] The *auto da fé* (Portuguese) or *auto de fé* (Spanish) referred to the public sentencing of those convicted of heresy. The term itself means act of faith. I have chosen to use the terms interchangeably as they appear in the source material.

2

The Inquisition in its Spanish and later Portuguese forms arose near the twilight of a long Jewish civilization in the Iberian Peninsula. For approximately the first forty years of the Spanish Inquisition, the primary concern was Judaizing. The term Judaizer was used to designate those Jewish converts to Christianity who had returned to Jewish practice. Occasionally, Old Christians who adopted Jewish practices or converted to Judaism were also tried as Judaizers. The problem was not new, and limited cases of Judaizing were reported in previous centuries. The difference was in the scale of the problem in the 12th and 13th centuries versus the 15th and 16th centuries.

The emergence of the Spanish Inquisition is tied to the tragic events which unfolded near the close of the 14th century in the Kingdoms of Castile and Aragon. After more than a thousand years of continual existence, in 1391, a new era in Jewish history began. Jewish communities throughout the Peninsula except those in the Kingdom of Portugal and the Kingdom of Granada were attacked en masse. Long-held Christian anti-Judaism and widespread political and economic discontent stoked the violence. The attacks forever altered the position of Jews in the Iberian Peninsula.

Thousands of Jews were murdered, and many more converted to Christianity under the direct threat of violence. The sheer scope of the attacks in 1391 overshadowed the severity of previous persecutions. The conversion of thousands of Jews initiated a social and religious crisis that lasted more than a century.

The Jews who converted to Christianity at the end of the 14th century and for the next one hundred years were known as Conversos in Christian literature and primarily as *anusim* i.e. forced converts in Jewish texts. Many of these converts retained Jewish practices. The continued observance of Jewish customs marked them as heretics. Since their initial conversions were under du-

3

ress, some Christians believed that leniency and time should be extended to them to embrace Christianity sincerely, but patience was wearing thin.

In 1478, King Ferdinand and Queen Isabella convinced Pope Sixtus IV to authorize a new Inquisition with unparalleled authority to search out lapsed converts. Pope Sixtus IV extended this authority in his bull titled *Exigit sincerae devotionis.* Inquisitional tribunals had existed in previous centuries, and local bishops had investigated Judaizing among Conversos as early as 1393 in the Kingdom of Aragon.[4] However, King Ferdinand and Queen Isabella saw Judaizing as spiritual cancer that required a national response. The previous Inquisitional tribunals headed by local bishops were seen as ineffective. The Pope granted this new Inquisition unique authority. The Inquisition was meticulous in its dealings and tried thousands of Conversos for heresy.

The Inquisition operated amidst the resentment that many Old Christians felt towards Conversos. Many Conversos had taken advantage of the new found social and economic opportunities open to them as Christians. The fact that many Conversos continued to practice Judaism secretly only heightened the hatred.

The Spanish Monarchs decided that despite the confiscation of property, imprisonment, and execution, the magnitude of Judaizing among Conversos was so high, that more action was needed. In 1492, frustrated with ongoing Judaizing practices, the Spanish monarchs ordered the expulsion of all unbaptized Jews.

According to King Ferdinand of Aragon and Queen Isabella of Castile, Judaizing by Conversos was the primary reason for

---

[4] In 1407, the Converso Jacme de Galiana was burned at the stake on the island of Majorca. He had lasped previously and was arrested again. Inquisitional activity was modest, however. Salo Wittmayer Baron, *A Social and the Religious History of the Jews: Volume XIII* (Philadelphia: Jewish Publication Society, 1969), 21.

4

their decision to order the expulsion of all unbaptized Jews from their Iberian and overseas dominions. The monarchs argued that some unbaptized Jews had aided and abetted Conversos in returning to the Jewish faith. The only way to resolve the problem was the absolute separation of the two groups.

Jews were given a choice between exile and conversion following King Ferdinand and Queen Isabella's conquest of the Kingdom of Granada in 1492. Faced with exile, many unbaptized Jews converted to Christianity adding to the already significant Converso class. More conversions were also brought about by the expulsion decrees issued by the Kingdom of Portugal in 1497 and the Kingdom of Navarre in 1498. Many exiles from Castile and Aragon took refuge in those domains in the wake of the original expulsion orders. These Jews believed they escaped conversion. They were dealt a fatal dose of reality.[5] Despite its perceived failure in definitively addressing Judaizing, the Spanish Inquisition continued its operations for more than three centuries. Those Jews who converted to forgo exile faced challenges with an anti-Converso sentiment very much alive despite the drastic moves already taken by the Spanish monarchs.

Amidst the tumultuous events which began in 1391 and ended in 1492, Portugal had been an almost veritable oasis. During the 14th and 15th century, the Jews of Portugal were spared violence. Thousands of Jews who found refuge there were forcibly baptized and forbidden to leave. The Portuguese Inquisition did not begin its operations for some time, but once they did, they had plenty of potential offenders.

This book provides a brief introduction to the rise of the Inquisition with a particular focus on the Church's concern over

---

[5] In 1502, King Ferdinand and Queen Isabella ordered the conversion of all Muslims residing in the Kingdom of Castile. The end goal was a united kingdom with a unified faith. Joseph Perez, *The Spanish Inquisition: A History* (London: Profile Books, 2006), 1.

Jews assisting converts to return to Judaism. This work also surveys the general history of the tribunal and provides information on the controversies and challenges presented by Inquisitional proceedings.

The first chapter, titled *Christianity and Forced Conversions* surveys the changing Christian views towards involuntary conversions. As the Crusader zeal spread, Jewish communities in France and Germany suffered attacks. Many individuals succumbed to the pressure and converted by force. Many Jews regretted their decision and tried to return to the Jewish community. The Church saw this as heresy, and the convert, as well as the Jews who assisted him or her in returning to Judaism, were subject to punishment.

The Church ultimately rejected forced conversions. The problem lay in conversions that had already taken place by violence. The Church determined that these conversions were irrevocable. Jews who converted to Christianity were forever Christians and subject to consequences for lapsing to Judaism.

The second chapter, titled *Assisting Relapsed Converts*, reviews the Jewish attempts to coax converts to Christianity to return to the Jewish fold. Various cases are documented in the medieval period. They were also commonplace in the era following the violence of 1391. The large scale conversions of Jews touched almost every Jewish family. Conversos lived in Jewish communities where their Jewish connections were reinforced, and their family members often continued their relationships with them.

The third chapter, titled *The Inquisition Reinvigorated*, relates the emergence of the Inquisition in Seville. King Ferdinand and Queen Isabella were convinced that Conversos were actively Judaizing. The Spanish Inquisition became the first modern institution with a sophisticated clerical organization. It was deliberate in its approach, and its power was largely unchecked.

The Inquisition faced a unique challenge in its prosecution of Judaizers. The problem lay in the changing nature of Converso attempts to retain some measure of Jewish identity.

The continued presence of non-converted Jews was vital to Conversos. Many of Conversos received religious and moral assistance from Jewish friends and family. As time passed, however, even the most sincere people intent on maintaining a Jewish identity were stymied by the gradual decline of Judaic knowledge. Contact with other Jews after the Expulsion was occasionally possible, but curious Conversos often gathered information regarding Judaism through the literature that the Inquisition itself had distributed to identify Judaizing practices.

The fourth chapter, titled *Edicts of Expulsion* concentrates on the decision of King Ferdinand and Queen Isabella to order the exile of all unbaptized Jews from their domains. By 1492 the Inquisition had prosecuted thousands of Conversos for Judaizing. While this progress was duly noted, the Monarchs believed the presence of Jews guaranteed that Conversos would continue to Judaize for generations. The way to implement a definitive solution to the problem was the expulsion of all Jews who refused to convert to Christianity. The goal was to cut Jewish knowledge at its source and hasten the demise of Judaizing among Conversos. The exile of unbaptized Jews virtually eliminated the influence Jews had on Conversos.

The fifth chapter, titled *The Kingdom of Portugal* discusses the unique situation for Jews and Conversos living there. The small Jewish community of Portugal survived intact for a century. The expulsion from Castile and Aragon brought tens of thousands of Jews to Portugal. For most Jews, Portugal was intended only to be a point of transit. A new round of forced conversions was ultimately enacted by royal decree to keep the Jewish community from leaving.

The sixth chapter titled *The Inquisition's Uncompromising Pursuit* reviews the institutions' continued work against heresy in the post-Expulsion era. After prosecuting thousands of Conversos, the Inquisition slowly redirected its energies to other threats like the Alumbrados and Protestantism.

The seventh chapter titled *The Inquisition in Portugal* returns to the topic of Portugal by discussing the rise of the tribunal in this kingdom. In contrast to Conversos in Castile and Aragon, Conversos or New Christians in Portugal were repeatedly spared the savagery of the Inquisition thanks to the successful lobbying of influential Conversos. Once the Portuguese Inquisition was finally established, it competed with its Spanish rival for cruelty.

The eighth chapter titled *Menasseh ben Israel and the Inquisition* discusses the case of Gaspar Rodrigues Nunes and his son, Manoel Dias Soeiro. The latter eventually escaped to the Jewish community of Amsterdam and became one of its rabbis. This chapter highlights this Inquisitional case and provides an example of the experience endured by its victims.

The last chapter, titled *Debating the Inquisition* provides a review of the dispute regarding the authenticity of Crypto-Judaism and the Inquisition records. Various scholars have questioned the validity of Inquisitional archives arguing that the incidents of purported Judaizing were effectively contrived. This chapter provides a review of the counter argument and why despite challenges, the Inquisition confirms the Crypto-Jewish experience.

The *Rise of the Inquisition* is a companion volume to my earlier book *Secret Jews: The Complex Identity of Crypto-Jews and Crypto-Judaism*. The latter work mentioned the Spanish and Portuguese Inquisition briefly as part of a historical overview of the Converso experience. I have however written the present work as a stand-alone volume for those who wish to focus more on the activities of the tribunal. There is an overlap of material in certain areas between the two works, but the overwhelming majority of the content in this book is not found in Secret Jews.

This volume is not intended as a comprehensive study of the Inquisition, but rather as an overview which illuminates key aspects of this institution that are often overlooked.

My goal is to provide the reader with information that will broaden his or her understanding of this fascinating as well as troubling era in history.

CHAPTER 1

Christianity and Forced Conversions

In the 4th century CE, the idea that conversion to Christianity must be voluntary and sincere was expressed in a law which forbade Jews from converting solely to escape their debts or crimes. Interestingly it is likely that some Jews in the 14th and 15th centuries converted exactly for this purpose. In the 5th century CE, the Church had even permitted Jewish converts to Christianity who were lax in their observance to return to Judaism if their conversions were known to have been motivated by reasons other than sincere faith. This position was ultimately rejected by the Visigoth King Alaric II and by the Fourth Council of Toledo in 633 CE.[1]

In the year 787 CE, the Second Council of Nicaea designated Jews who had been baptized but continued to observe Jewish practices or maintain Jewish beliefs as non-Christians. Pope

---

[1] The work titled the Breviarium, a collection of Roman law disseminated in 506 CE, was written under King Alaric II 's direction. Ammon Linder, *The Jews in Roman Imperial Legislation* (Detroit: Wayne State University Press, 1987), 199-200.

Adrian I rejected this view.[2] In 1144, King Louis VII of France declared that many Jews had undergone baptism but returned to Judaism at the prompting of the devil. These individuals were to suffer exile, corporal punishment, or even death.[3] In 1171, after many Jews were killed in the city of Blois in central France, Jews were successful in bribing the archbishop of Sens to allow those who had been forcibly converted to Christianity to return to Judaism.[4]

John Gratian Author of the Decretum

In the twelfth century, experts in canon law framed new rulings regarding forced baptism. They did so based on the earlier Fourth Council of Toledo. Pope Calixtus II affirmed this in his

---

[2] Edward Synan, *The Popes and the Jews in the Middle Ages* (New York: Macmillan, 1965), 55, 58

[3] Despite the apparent support of other Jews in the apostates' return to Judaism, no threats were levied against the Jewish community Leopold Delisle, ed. *Recuiel de Historeigns des Gaules et de la France* (Farnborough: Gregg International Publishers, 1968), Vol. 16. p.8, no 19.

[4] Those assisting lapsed converts return to Judaism did not face punishment. Edward Fram, "Perception and Reception of Repentant Apostates in Medieval Ashkenaz and Premodern Poland," AJS Review 21/2 (1996): 303.

bull titled Sicut Judeis that no Jew was to be converted by force. Those who had been, however, were not allowed to leave the Christian fold.[5] The Christian theologian John Gratian (circa 1140) in his work titled Decretum stated the following principle that became the model for Western Christendom.

"Those, however, who had already been compelled- as in the days of the very religious prince, Sisebut-inasmuch as by accepting the grace of baptism they had become associated with the divine sacraments...it is only proper that they be compelled to retain the faith they accepted, whether by force or necessity, lest the name of the Lord be blasphemed and the faith they had assumed be considered vile and contemptible."[6]

Nadia Zeldes summarizes the changes in the Church's approach to the forced conversions of Jews.

"The new rulings distinguished between absolute coercion and conditional coercion. Absolute coercion was interpreted as a situation whereby a person was physically restrained (i.e. held by another and tied down) so that there was nothing that person could do to prevent the pouring of holy water. Only, in that case, an unwilling Jew was not to be constrained to hold to the Christian faith. But in conditional coercion, that is, whenever a person was being threatened with death unless he consented to be baptized, there was, they argued, an element of free choice and that individual should be constrained to hold the faith."[7]

---

[5] Ibid., 304.

[6] Ibid., 305.

[7] Nadia Zeldes, "Legal Status of Jewish Converts to Christianity to Southern Italy and Provence," California Italian Studies Journal, Vol.I:I (2010): 7.

Pope Innocent III also accepted the difference between conditional and absolute compulsion. In 1201 he stated that if a person were dragged violently by torture and accepted baptism to "avoid loss" they would nevertheless have received the "impressed character of Christianity" as would the individual who feigned conversion.[8] Both were to be compelled to observe Christianity "...as one conditionally willing."[9] As Edward Fram notes, besides openly choosing death when threatened with forced conversion, there was very little any Jew could do to persuade the Church that they did not want to convert.[10]

Concomitant with this, the Franciscan monk, Ramon Llull (1233-1316) argued that the resolution to the Jewish menace lay in the outright proscription of Judaism. Llull argued that since Christianity was the only true religious faith, Jews who refused to adopt it should be expelled from Christian lands. The pres-

---

[8] "...drawn to Christianity by violence, through fear and through torture, and received the sacrament of baptism in order to avoid loss." Edward Fram, "Perception and Reception of Repentant Apostates in Medieval Ashkenaz and Premodern Poland," AJS Review 21/2 (1996): 305.

[9] According to Pope Innocent III, the individual who is baptized even under torture "...does receive the impress of Christianity and may be forced to observe the Christian Faith as one who expressed a conditional willingness though, absolutely speaking, he was unwilling. ... [For] the grace of Baptism had been received, and they had been anointed with the sacred oil, and had participated in the body of the Lord, they might properly be forced to hold to the faith which they had accepted perforce, lest the name of the Lord be blasphemed, and lest they hold in contempt and consider vile the faith they had joined." Solomon Grayzel, The Church and the Jews in the Thirteenth Century, rev. ed. (New York: Hermon, 1966), 103.

[10] Edward Fram, "Perception and Rerception of Repentant Apostates in Medieval Ashkenaz and Premodern Poland," AJS Review 21/2 (1996): 305.

ence of professing Jews on Christian lands was a threat to the Church.[11]

Lull's views were reinforced by the Dominican Friar Ramon Marti (1220-1286). Marti believed that those Jews who had embraced Christianity were in danger of succumbing to the influences of Jews to return to Judaism. The only solution was the physical separation of Jews and these converts. As a consequence, tolerating Judaism guaranteed that it would flourish and present temptation to converts to return to their Jewish ways. Despite the changing attitudes, there was still a recognition that forced conversions were problematic. Much later, one of the prominent commentators on the works of Thomas Aquinas, Tommaso de Vio, a general of the Dominican order, highlighted the problems.

"...threats and terror wherewith the princes force their subjects to embrace the faith result only in their servile, rather than voluntary, conversion and hence in sacrilege...For to receive the sacraments under force is to bring contumely upon them...It certainly is a greater evil to live secretly as an unbeliever after having received the sacraments of the faith than to live freely as an infidel, for thus one avoids [at least] the contumely to the sacraments."[12]

---

[11] The infamous Fray Diego de Marchena from Guadalupe visited Seville a number of times and interacted with the Jewish community there. On one occasion he entered a synagogue and presented a letter to the rabbi given to him by an imprisoned Jew. Several members of his own family tried to escape to Granada to practice Judaism openly. Fray Diego worked to have them released. Gretchen D. Starr-LeBeau, *In the Shadow of the Virgin: Inquisitors, Friars, and Conversos in Guadalupe, Spain* (Princeton, Princeton University Press, 2003), 216.

[12] Salo Witmayer Baron, *Social and Religious History of the Jews, Volume IX* (New York: Columbia University Press, 1965), 12.

Las Siete Partidas and Alfonso X of Castile

Las Siete Partidas, a law code written in Castilian and compiled around 1265, under the direction of King Alfonso X, the Wise (1252-1284) of Castile also referred to the issue of coerced conversion.

"No force or compulsion shall be employed in any way against a Jew to induce him to become a Christian;but Christians should convert him to the faith of Our Lord Jesus Christ by means of the texts of the Holy Scriptures, and by kind words, for no one can love or appreciate a service which is done him by compulsion. We also decree that if any Jew or Jewess should voluntarily desire to become a Christian, the other Jews shall not interfere with this in any way, and if they stone, wound, or kill any such person, because he wished to become a Christian, or after he has been baptized, and this can be proved; we order that all the murderers, or the abettors of said murder or attack, shall be burned. [This law was first issued by Constantine the Great in 315] But where the party was not killed, but wounded, or dishonored; we order the judges of the neighborhood where this took place shall

15

compel those guilty of the attack, or who caused the dishonor, to make amends to him for the same; and also that they be punished for the offence which the committed, as they think they deserve; and we also order that, after any Jews become Christians, all persons in our dominions shall honor them; and that no one shall dare to reproach them or their descendants, by way of insult, with having been Jews; and that they shall possess all their property, sharing the same with their brothers and inheriting it from their fathers and mothers and other relatives just as if they were Jews; and that they can hold all offices and dignities which other Christians can do."[13]

Interestingly, the Las Siete Partidas were not adopted as authoritative law until at around 1348. This was a little more than 40 years before the violence of 1391 which transformed the Iberian Peninsula forever and spelled the doom of the Jewish community.

In 1277 several Jewish converts to Christianity who returned to Judaism were burned by order of Pope Nicolas III. Thirteen Jews were also burned as heretics in 1288 in the city of Troyes. In 1299 the Jews in Rome protested to Pope Boniface VIII that the inquisitors would not reveal the names of either witnesses or those accusing them. The Pope responded positively and protected Jews from this. In Paris March 31, 1310, a converted Jew who had returned to Judaism was also burned by order of the Inquisition.

---

[13] Jacob Marcus, *The Jew in the Medieval World: A Sourcebook, 315-1791* (New York: JPS, 1938), 34-42.

Pope Gregory X

The Papal Inquisition initially created to deal with the Albigenses gradually spread in southern France and into the Kingdom of Aragon. In 1233 Pope Gregory X directed Archbishop of Tarragona to assign inquisitors. By the 14th century, Aragon had a Grand Inquisitor. The Inquisition's jurisdiction over lapsed converts was confirmed in 1359 when several Jews who had returned to Judaism fled from Provence to Spanish territory. King Pedro IV of Aragon authorized the inquisitor Bernard du Puy to punish them appropriately when captured.

The Inquisition also saw activity on the island of Sicily. Under the reign of Emperor Frederick II, the Inquisition began operations in 1224. It was allowed to receive one-third of the property confiscated from Jews. In 1344, the Pope Clement VI gave authority to his legate in Naples to punish all Jewish apostates. In 1355 Pope Innocent VI instructed Francisco da Messina to carry out his responsibilities thoroughly. Persecuted and deprived of their property, in 1375, Jews appealed for relief to the King. The King responded by ordering that the Inquisitors keep prisoners in royal prisons only. They were also required to have local judges take part in the prosecution. The condemned had the right to appeal.

Pope Nicolas V's appointment of Matteo da Reggio as an inquisitor in 1449 highlights the continuing focus of the Inquisition on lapsed Jewish apostates. The Pope directed da Reggio to execute converted Jews guilty of lapsing to Judaism. In 1451 Curio Lugardi, the inquisitor of Palermo obliged the Jewish community to contribute to the service of the inquisitor and for his official traveling expenses once a year.

CHAPTER 2

Assisting Lapsed Converts

The punishment imposed on those who helped lapsed converts to return to Judaism varied. In Southern Italy in early 1290, a Jew who supported a lapsed convert was fined. The punishment might have been much more severe if the medieval Inquisition were involved.[1] Lapsed converts often underwent a process of rejudaization. The rituals they underwent were not technically required by Jewish law but were practiced by some French and German Jewish communities.[2] These rituals were designed to remove the stain that baptism had purportedly brought to the body of the Jew and restore religious purity.[3] French Inquisitional authorities sought the extradition of the lapsed converts and requested that local governments take action against those who assisted them. By 1311, the Inquisition operating in Aragon launched investigations against Jews who offered help to lapsed converts. Rumors that Jews in Majorca were also supporting lapsed converts placed the safety of the Majorcan Jewish community at risk.[4]

Despite such action, Jewish communities in Aragon extended lapsed converts safe haven.[5] In 1306, King Philip IV ordered that all unbap-

---

[1] Edward Fram, "Perception and Reception of Repentant Apostates in Medieval Ashkenaz and Premodern Poland," AJS Review 21/2 (1996): 311.

[2] Ibid., 311.

[3] Joseph Shatzmiller, "Converts and Judaizers in Early Fourteenth Century," Harvard Theological Review 74, no.1 (1981): 63-66, 69.

[4] Yitzhak Baer, A History of the Jews in Christian Spain Volume II, (Philadelphia: Jewish Publication Society, 1961), 10.

[5] Edward Fram, "Perception and Reception of Repentant Apostates in Medieval Ashkenaz and Premodern Poland," AJS Review 21/2 (1996): 312.

tized Jews leave France. Many Jews traveled crossed the Pyrenees Mountains and entered into Catalonia where King James II of Aragon allowed them to settle. King Louis X, who succeeded Philip IV, allowed Jews to settle in France anew in 1315.[6] In 1320 and 1321, many Jews apostatized to Christianity during the violence instigated by the Shepherds crusade. Many converts entered the Kingdom of Aragon and openly returned to Judaism with some local assistance.

Jewish Attempts at Rejudaizing Converts

Bernard Gui described lapsed converts as returning to the vomit of Judaism. These lapsed converts were guilty regardless of whether they were voluntary converts or had converted under duress. Regarding the assistance Jews extended to lapsed converts, Gui wrote:

"The perfidious Jews attempt, when and wherever they can, secretly to pervert Christians and to attract them to the Jewish perfidy. They do it particularly in the case of those who had been Jews, but were converted and accepted baptism and the Christian faith; and most especially those related to them by marriage or blood. It is ordained, however, that the procedure against Christians going over or returning to the Jews' rite- the latter even if baptized as infants or through the fear of death but not under absolute and positive force- shall be the same as heretics, whether they themselves confess or are convicted, through [the testimony of] Christians or Jews. Their patrons, receivers, and defenders, too, are to be treated on a par with such abettors of heretics."[7]

In 1321, Bernard Gui in his inquisitorial manual Practica oficii inquisitionis heretice pravitatis asserted that Jews actively wanted to rejudaize Jewish converts. They did so secretly, and from Gui's perspective, this threatened the Church and Christian society. Gui attempted to pro-

---

[6] Only a few years later, in 1322, Charles IV again issued an edict of Expulsion. Kristine T. Utterback, "Conversi-Revert: Voluntary and Forced Return to Judaism in the Early Fourteenth Century," Church History, Vol. 64. No. I (1995): 16.

[7] Salo Wittmayer Baron, A Social and the Religious History of the Jews: Volume XIII (Philadelphia: Jewish Publication Society, 1969), 9.

vide inquisitors with the tools and guidelines for identifying Judaizers and the apostates in his manual.[8]

Pope Clement IV's bull titled Turbato corde in 1267 had already defined (re)Judaizing as heresy. Gui considered all Jews as a potential threat to the Church as evidenced by the fact that they cursed Christians in their liturgy. They also held blasphemous views on Jesus and Mary. While all Jews posed a threat, those Judaizers were direct supporters of heresy, encouraging the convert to relapse.

Gui's account of reversion to Judaism was also confirmed by other fourteenth century inquisitors who tried Judaizers.[9]

Shepherds' Crusaders Killing 500 Jews at Verdun-sur-Garonne in 1320

The Case of Salves Barbe

Salves Barbe was a Jew arrested by the Inquisition for aiding a convert return to Judaism. The incident likely occurred under the Inquisitional supervision of the Franciscan monk, Bertrand de Cigoterio.

---

[8] Kristine T. Utterback, "Conversi-Revert: Voluntary and Forced Return to Judaism in the Early Fourteenth Century," Church History, Vol. 64. No. I (1995): 17.

[9] Ibid., 18.

Cigoterio served as the inquisitor of Provence in 1283 and acted as a principal inquisitor in 1290 for the Combat Venaissan. Salves Barbe was interrogated and asked if he had participated in a return ceremony of a lapsed convert.

Salves Barbe faced testimony from a lapsed convert named Johannes. Salves was tortured and confessed. Johannes contacted the Jewish community and expressed his regret for having converted. He was apparently convincing enough for several Jews to help him. Johannes met Salves Barbe and other Jews on a designated Friday. Johannes underwent an initial immersion in the sea and then the second one in hot water. Salves Barbes was let off easily with only a promise to never participate in such a ritual again. [10]

Not all Jewish communities reacted as openly to returning converts. The Jewish communities in German lands were more reserved than those in Aragon. A lapsed convert in German lands had greater opportunity to minimize the danger to the Jewish community if he or she fled to another region. In fact, in the aftermath of the Rindfleisch persecutions, some Jews journeyed as far as Spain or Italy. The Jews of Aragon may have determined that there were no other regions to which they could realistically send returning apostates.

The communities of Aragon were forced to make a determination to either confront the danger of assisting returning converts or leave them to their own devices and within the Christian fold. It was a choice which offered no ideal solution. As time progressed, the sheers numbers of conversions contrasted the situation of returning apostates in German lands and those in Spanish ones. To highlight the significance of this, Edward Fram notes that for German Jewry,

"Historical events did not challenge their belief that the welfare of the Jewish community outweighed the spiritual welfare of individual apostates. The Jews of Aragon did not have this luxury." [11]

---

[10] Joseph Shatzmiller, "Converts and Judaizers in Early Fourteenth Century," Harvard Theological Review 74, no.1 (1981): 69-70.

[11] Edward Fram, "Perception and Reception of Repentant Apostates in Medieval Ashkenaz and Premodern Poland," AJS Review 21/2 (1996): 313. The Jews of Germany appear to have also been particularly concerned with the practice of some returning apostates to incur punishment on the Jewish community

The danger of Christian retribution for assisting lapsed converts was already recorded in *Sefer Hasidim* which was written in the 13th century.

"And if there is an apostate, and it is known to the important people in the town and the sages in the town that he is willing to repent, but if he flees there will be a danger to the people [i.e., Jews] of the town because [the Christians] will say that the Jews caused him to flee, then he can fool the non-Jews and say that he wants to go on a pilgrimage. And he should take upon him the cross until he leaves the place where people know him and [then] remove [the cross] and there will be no complaints against the Jews."[12]

If the lapsed convert presented a potential threat to the community because of their profile or possible escape, it was better to forgo any support or contact with them. Regardless of their sincerity, it was better to have nothing to do with a person that could cause injury to other Jews.[13]

The Case of Johannes

The Inquisitional records of Gui in 1317 discuss the case of Johannes de Bretz. Johannes was from Toulouse and converted to Christianity. He lived as a Christian for three years. He then fled to Lerida where he un-

---

on the basis of false accusations. In the case of Reichart of Mospach, he switched identities repeatedly with the purpose of stealing from both Jews and Christians and taking advantage of women along the way. Most importantly, he accused the Jews of Krautheim and Bamberg of having bought and extracted blood from the host. Such occurrences reinforced the weariness of German Jewry towards returning converts and vacillating individuals. Ibid. 314.

[12] Edward Fram, "Perception and Reception of Repentant Apostates in Medieval Ashkenaz and Premodern Poland," AJS Review 21/2 (1996): 306.

[13] In a case involving a non-Jewish girl who converted to Judaism, eventually converted to Christianity and then desired to return to Judaism, she was sent to the Hungarian village of Irek where she was unknown and could hide more successfully. According to Rabbi Isaac ben Moses of Vienna, had she been caught, she would have been executed. Edward Fram, "Perception and Reception of Repentant Apostates in Medieval Ashkenaz and Premodern Poland," AJS Review 21/2 (1996): 307, 309.

derwent a rejudaizing ritual. The local authorities learned of the situation and deported him to Toulouse. He refused to recant and returned to Judaism. As a result, he was sentenced by Gui to life imprisonment. The same year, Gui also tried another lapsed Jew. This trial was posthumous, however. The case involved the case of another individual also named Johannes (his name was Josse when a Jew). He had relapsed to Judaism and when confronted with his lapse refused to recant.[14]

The Case of Baruch

In 1320, Bishop Jacques Fournier of Pamiers tried a case of a convert reverting to Judaism. This convert claimed he converted under duress. Baruch, the Jewish convert, was attacked by members of the Shepherd's Crusade. Members of this group were tried in Toulouse for having killed one hundred and fifty Jews at Castel Sarassin. The accused had been set free by bystanders as they were escorted to the Narbonne Fort. Upon their freedom, they ransacked the Jewish quarter. During the violence, a group of peasants bursts into the room where Baruch had been studying and required that he either convert or die.[15]

Faced with the choice, Baruch acceded to conversion. A Christian friend advised him to go to Pamiers so he could resume his Jewish practice. Baruch testified to the existence of a procedure for converted Jews returning to Judaism but explained that since his conversion was under duress, there was no need for such a process. He fled but was arrested by the Inquisition on the charge of returning to Judaism. Bishop Jacques Fournier found Baruch's argument unconvincing. Because Baruch had not "protested by word or deed or shown a contrary will, by resisting, that he did not want to be baptized." The Inquisitors, of course, failed to admit that any such protestation would have likely resulted in Baruch's death. Consequently, Bishop Fournier refused to declare the baptism invalid.[16]

---

[14] Joseph Shatzmiller, "Converts and Judaizers in the Early Fourteenth Century," HTR, Vol. 74, No 1. (1981): 67.

[15] Yosef H. Yerushalmi, "The Inquisition and the Jews of France in the time of Bendard Gui," HTR 63 (1970): 328.

[16] Yosef H. Yerushalmi, "The Inquisition and the Jews of France in the time of Bendard Gui," HTR 63 (1970): 330.

Fourier argued that only total coercion made the sacrament of baptism void. This was despite the fact that Baruch had told him that his captors told him that if he protested it would have meant certain death. Left with no other options, Baruch opted to confess his guilt. Once again he abjured Judaism. The two other cases discussed are not recorded as having been forced.[17]

Bernard Gui details this rejudaization process in his Inquisitional manual. The procedure known as *Judeorum ritus et modus in rejudaysando conversos baptizatos* included the following elements:

"The rite or mode of the Jews in rejudaizing baptized converts who return to the vomit of Jerusalem is as follows: He who is to be rejudaized is summoned and asked by one of the Jews present whether he wishes to submit to what is called tymla [tebila] in Hebrew, which in Latin means whether he wished to take a bath or washing in running water, in order to become a Jew. He replies that he does. Then the Jew who presided says to him in Hebrew Baaltussuna (=baal-tesuba) which means in Latin, 'you are reverting from the state of sin.' After this, he is stripped of his garments and is sometimes bathed in warm water. The Jews then rub him energetically with sand over his entire body, but especially on his forehead, chest, and arms that are on the places which during baptism received the holy chrism. Then they cut the nails of his hands and feet until they bleed. They shave his head, and afterward put him in the waters of a flowing stream, and plunge his head into the water three times. After this immersion, they recite the following prayer: 'Blessed be God, the Lord eternal, who has commanded us to sanctify ourselves in this water or bath which called tyvila (sic) in Hebrew." This done, he emerges from the water, dons a new shirt and breeches, and all the attending Jews kiss him and give him a name, which is usually the name he had before baptism. He who is thus rejudaized is required to confess his belief in the Law of Moses, to promise to keep and observe it and to live henceforth according to it. Similarly, that he renounces baptism and the Christian faith, and that henceforth he will

---

[17] Joseph Shatzmiller, "Converts and Judaizers in the Early Fourteenth Century," HTR, Vol. 74, No 1. (1981): 67.

neither keep nor serve it. And he promised to observe the Law and repudiate baptism and the Christian faith. Afterward, they give him a certificate or testimonial letter to all other Jews so that they may receive him, trust him, and assist him. From then on he lives and acts a Jew and attends the School, or Synagogue, of the Jews."[18]

Bernard Gui's description reveals what was tantamount to a counter baptism evidenced by the rigorous washing of areas that had made contact with baptismal waters.[19] Gui's description of the dechristianization ritual is also corroborated by the testimony of the previously mentioned lapsed convert Johannes de Bretz.[20]

In 1341, in the city of Barcelona, three Jews were accused by the Inquisition of rejudaizing a lapsed convert. On August 11, 1342, following an investigation, judgment was rendered against Janto Almuli, his wife Jamila, and Jucef de Quartortze. All three Jews were from La Almunia de la Godinda, near Calatayud. They were convicted for helping to rejudaize a Converso named Peter. Jucef was also charged with helping bring about the death of another convert named Abadia.

Janto was sentenced to perpetual imprisonment, and his rations set as bread and water. His wife Jamila was also sentenced to perpetual imprisonment. Jucef had been previously convicted of circumcising a Christian boy. Whether the boy was the son of a Jewish man or woman who had converted to Christianity is unclear.[21]

This earlier case made Jucef a relapsed heretic despite his Jewish status. Jucef was sentenced to death and burned. During their incarceration and before their sentencing, the Dominican Bernat de Puigcercos question the three. Peter, who had been known as Alatzar before his conver-

---

[18] Yosef H. Yerushalmi, "The Inquisition and the Jews of France in the time of Bendard Gui," HTR 63 (1970): 363-364.

[19] Joseph Shatzmiller, "Converts and Judaizers in the Early Fourteenth Century," HTR, Vol. 74, No 1. (1981): 64.

[20] According to Kristine Utterback, the returning apostate received a certificate stating that he was a Jew and was received back into the Jewish community. Kristine T. Utterback, "Conversi-Revert: Voluntary and Forced Return to Judaism in the Early Fourteenth Century," Church History, Vol. 64. No. 1 (1995): 20.

[21] Ibid., 21-22.

sion, admitted that his adoption of Christianity was a personal choice. He said divine inspiration led him to seek baptism.

After being baptized at the Church of Sant Pere de Riudebittles close to the city of Barcelona, he headed to the Diocese of Tarazona, in Calatayud where he planned to live a Christian life. During the first part of his journey, he stayed with Christians. As he continued, he remained with Jews. After eight days, Peter arrived at La Alumina where he stayed with Salmon Navarro and his wife Miriam who were Jewish. Peter declared that he had become a Christian.

Salomon was extremely distraught since even eating with a Christian could bring him before the Inquisition as a supporter of apostasy. Nonetheless, he allowed Peter to stay with them since he had known him previously. The following day, Salomon sent Peter to a Jew named Janto Almuli. Almuli ran a transportation business which would allow Peter to get a ride to Calatayud. Janto attempted to convince Peter to renounce Christianity and return to Judaism.[22]

An alternate version of the story claimed that Navarros had taken Peter to Janto's house where several Jewish elders were waiting. They attempted to convince Peter to bring about his death to save his soul, in what may have been ritual suicide or something akin to it, in the vein of kiddush ha-shem, the sanctification of the LORD's name.

At Janto's house, Peter heard the account of Abadia who had also become a Christian. Abadia was also convinced to lapse to Judaism. Convinced of the error of his actions, Abadia had turned himself over to the civil authorities in Calatayud. Under their authority, he expected to be burned to save his soul. Janto or the council attempted to convince Peter to do the same. Janto apparently stated:

> "O you poor wretch, how could you have erred so greatly that you abandoned the law of Moses, the law of the one and true God, and accepted the Christian law, which is vain and dead, and by which you can never be saved?"[23]

Janto explained that if Peter were willing to die, his death would count as martyrdom before God. He would achieve salvation for his martyrdom. Abadia was told that he was also required to abolish all hints of his baptism. This included removing the skin from his forehead,

---

[22] Ibid., 22.
[23] Ibid., 23.

and from anywhere the oil had been applied during baptism. This included his knees, and he was also required to cut off the tips of the fingers he used to make the sign of the cross. Peter was expected to do the same. Peter retired to the Navvaros' home to contemplate what decision he would take. Peter ultimately decided to turn himself over to the civil authorities. He renounced Christianity and was sentenced to death. At the point of being burned, some Dominicans intervened and saved him.

People Burned as Heretics

Kristine Utterback theorizes this was in return for his testimony against the Jewish community. The case of the lapsed convert Abadia was entirely different. He was executed in Calatayud by the civil authorities. The Inquisition also charged Janto for coaxing Peter and Abadia to return to Judaism. Regarding the rejudaizing of Peter, Janto initially denied all the charges. Eventually, Janto broke down and confessed to the majority of the accusations, though not to have instructed Peter on what to say. He denied that he had been involved with the Abadia's lapse. In the end, Janto's statement implicated others, in particular, Jucef.

Jucef and Janto's wife Jamila were also questioned and punished. The matter of a Jew converting to Christianity and then relapsing to Judaism was an issue the Church took quite seriously. The Jews of La Almunia in the kingdom of Aragon also saw this as a far-reaching matter and were willing to go to great lengths to bring someone back to Judaism. The penance they expected, however, was quite severe and could even include martyrdom via the condemnation of the Christian civil authorities.[24]

---

[24] Ibid., 24.

Early Inquisitional Tribunals in Aragon

In the aftermath of the violence of 1391 and the ensuing conversions that followed in the 15th century, the Converso community of Castile and Aragon was as Maria Dolores Cabanas describes a "mixed bag of pseudo-converts, apostates, crypto-Jews, etc. which became a rich tilling ground for the new Inquisition..." The Conversos, whatever their true intent were bound to "hover permanently close to the" edge separating orthodoxy from heresy.[25]

Distinctive Badges on English Jews

In 1396, King Joan of Aragon was apprised that Conversos in Morvedre near Valencia were still living with Jews as they had before they had been baptized. These Conversos were indistinguishable from Jews since Jews and Christians dressed alike. The scholar Mark Meyerson relates the concern King Joan expressed towards this reality.

"The danger of this state of affairs for the conversos and even for the Old Christians was patent. Joan, therefore, issued prohibitions against the conversos' living with Jews, or eating, drinking, and praying with them. Since it was necessary that the Jews be easily identifiable, he required them to wear a red badge on their clothing. This last measure was intended not to harass the Jews, whose

---

[25] Joaquim Carvalho ed., *Religion and Power in Europe: Conflict and Convergence* (Pisa: Edizioni Plus - Pisa University Press, 2007), 79.

29

recovery and prosperity the Crown encouraged, but to inhibit the backsliding of conversos."[26]

Upon the death of King Joan in 1396, his brother Marti I ascended the throne. King Marti I recognized that the conversions of 1391 had taken place under violent circumstances. Furthermore, Conversos were not given the opportunity to receive instruction in their new faith, nor did they possess any desire or enthusiasm for doing so. They were then, susceptible if not embracing of the persuasions and reinforcements of Jewish identity proffered by their Jewish families and friends.[27] Decades later, the lack of eagerness by many Conversos to practice Christianity was still evident. Fray Alonso de Nogales, from Guadalupe, noted Converso behavior during a Mass.

"...many were in attendance...and as I knew that there were conversos among them, at the time that the priest raised the Lord above his head I, because of the suspicions I had of them, stood up and toward the ground; and I was quite disturbed by this and I began to say bad things about conversos and to be much more suspicious about their acts and lives."[28]

---

[26] Mark D. Meyerson, *A Jewish Renaissance in Fifteenth-Century Spain* (Princeton: Princeton University Press, 2004), 42. In the second half of the 15th century, Mari Gonzalez from Guadalupe reported that Fray Lope de Villarael had delivered a disturbing message during her confessional. "...one day confessing herself with fray Lope de Villareal he asked her some things concerning confession. And as the good woman did not know how to respond to what he asked, fray Lope the confessor said, 'Although he is considered a heretic, Fernan Gonzalez the scrivener knows how to answer better than you. Well then, what is raised at the altar?' The old woman replied, 'What is raised at the altar is the true body and blood of Our Lord Jesus Christ,' to which he responded, 'It is nothing but bread and wine.' And when she heard this and many other things she did not agree with she began to cry out strongly that he would not make her become Jewish. And so having heard this she never confessed with him again." Gretchen D. Starr-LeBeau, *In the Shadow of the Virgin: Inquisitors, Friars, and Conversos in Guadalupe, Spain* (Princeton, Princeton University Press, 2003), 220-221.

[27] Mark D. Meyerson, *A Jewish Renaissance in Fifteenth-Century Spain* (Princeton: Princeton University Press, 2004), 42.

[28] Gretchen D. Starr-LeBeau, *In the Shadow of the Virgin: Inquisitors, Friars, and Conversos in Guadalupe, Spain* (Princeton, Princeton University Press, 2003), 64.

King Marti I of Aragon

To counter the effect of Jews interacting with Conversos, on February 22, 1397, King Marti prohibited the reconstruction of the Jewish Quarter and ordered the expulsion of all remaining Jews in the city of Valencia. Jews were to exit the city within 20 days and settle in Morvedre and other towns. The problem of Conversos continuing to practice Judaism was of course not resolved by the expulsion of Jews from the city of Valencia. While over public displays may have been problematic, the Conversos of Valencia were still knowledgeable enough to observe Judaism without them.

With this is mind, King Marti on February 4th, 1398, ordered Guillem de Feriaria, a royal official to work with the papal inquisitor to eliminate Judaizing among Conversos. Conversos were prohibited from consorting with Jews. The even minimal interaction was considered dangerous.[29] As part of the effort, the episcopal vicar of Valencia or-

---

[29] The case of Manuel Gonzalez from the town of Guadalupe likely demonstrates how Conversos asked practicing Jews traveling through the area for Jewish instruction. Gonzalez was an inn keeper. He was arrested by the Inquisition and a hand written prayer book was found in his possession. According to Starr-LeBeau, "It is likely that he used his position as innkeeper to ask traveling Jews to write down remembered prayers as ell. Except for the inclusion of the word Adonay for God, all prayers were in Spanish with Roman letters and appear to be either remembered prayers of penitence and petitions for aid or variations on the Psalms." Gonzalez was sufficiently learned in Jewish practice to recite a beracha (blessing) at meals and ran a kosher kitchen. Gretchen D. Starr-LeBeau, *In the Shadow of the Virgin: Inquisitors, Friars, and Conversos in Guadalupe, Spain* (Princeton, Princeton University Press, 2003), 60-61, 85.

dered that all Christians cease purchasing kashered meat, stop attending Jewish or Muslim weddings, desist from lighting candles, and stop preparing food in the homes of Jews on the Sabbath.[30]

In 1400, King Marti was apprised that the Inquisition in Xativa had ceased prosecuting Conversos. Local notables had approached the inquisitors. They had also received a nominal bribe of 500 *sous* by some Conversos who were potential targets of their investigation. Several Converso families had also been actively converting their property into silver and jewelry so they could escape to North Africa. A royal official named Guillem Martorell was sent by King Marti to confiscate the property of these families and to arrest them as well. Martorell was ordered to reprove the Inquisition to continue with its prosecution.[31]

Almost a decade after the forced conversions, Conversos continued to practice Jewish customs, and this appears to have puzzled King Marti. Like his brother, he could not grasp how baptized Jews could not embrace the truth of Christianity. Mark Meyerson notes that in contrast to King Joan, King Marti focused on the Talmud as the source of the obfuscation. Meyerson states:

> "The Talmud, the king, concluded still rendered the Jews blind to the scriptural evidence of Jesus's messianic status; it was having the same effect on conversos who consorted with Talmudic Jews. In almost a postscript to this pragmatic of August 1400 prohibiting the conversos' Jewish practices, Marti called on his officials to see that the sentences of Gregory Innocent concerning the Talmud were observed. The king presumably had in mind the confiscation and examination and perhaps even the burning – of Talmudic texts."[32]

King Marti effectively blamed Jews for spreading Talmudic heresy among Conversos. For this, he authorized all officials to assist inquisitors in their current or future investigation against Jews and Saracens and their agents.[33] King Marti's zeal to end Judaizing by Conversos by prosecuting Jews began to produce unintended consequences. Marti

---

[30] Mark D. Meyerson, *A Jewish Renaissance in Fifteenth-Century Spain* (Princeton: Princeton University Press, 2004), 43.

[31] Ibid., 44.

[32] Ibid., 44.

[33] Ibid., 45.

wanted his Jewish community to flourish economically. The Inquisition, though, was now damaging the King's property and his royal coffers.

In another case, a noted Jew, Jacob Facan was accused of having maligned the Catholic faith. Queen Maria cognizant of the negative impact that a successful prosecution would cause, intervened to block the inquisitors. Mark Meyerson states:

> "She chose to disregard the fact that five years earlier Jacob had been accused of delivering matzah to the conversos of Sogorb and convicted for sending his baptized son to North Africa. It mattered less to Maria that Jacob might possibly have encouraged conversos to Judaize that that 'our rights and our vassals…will remain whole."[34]

The Inquisition adopted an odd approach to the Converso dilemma. Instead of prosecuting Jews for assisting Conversos to Judaize, the Inquisition pursued Jews they claimed had been baptized and were now claiming to have never been. Once accusation was made against Jamila, the daughter of the well-do-to Jew of Valencia named Jahuda Alatzar. The accusation though was made by the Converso Manuel Salvador in a purportedly sordid plot which the Queen argued was based on Salvador's desire for Jamila to marry his Converso brother in law.[35] If true, the charges were not borne out of any animosity between the Conversos and Jews as a class, but rather as the result of the machinations of Manuel Salvador.

Mark Meyerson sees these accusations as completely false, but the Inquisition may have opted for a sophisticated strategy to terrorize Jews to have them leave the kingdom. With Jews actively assisting Conversos, their departure may have been considered as a long-term solution to the Converso dilemma. In the end, Queen Maria intervened and ordered the inquisitors to cease these actions.

While King Marti grew appalled at the inquisitional tactics regarding professing Jews, the matter of Judaizing Conversos was still an issue of grave concern for him. In December 1401, he ordered lay officials to examine charges that the Converso, Jaume de Lorde was consorting with Jews and "turning to [their] customs, rites, and observances." Despite the reprimands from the Crown, the Aragonese inquisition restart-

---

[34] Ibid., 47.
[35] Ibid., 50.

ed its operations against Jews in the summer of 1404. The support of Hug de Llupia, the Bishop of Valencia, strengthened the Inquisition in its attack against Jews.[36] Queen Maria continued to intervene in the Inquisition's attempted prosecution of Jews. It appears that she tried to bring about a conciliation regarding the methods of investigation and appropriate punishments for Jews in Morvedre. As Meyerson states:

"If the queen was willing to admit that perhaps some Jews deserved punishment, then presumably some Jews had been conniving in the Judaizing of conversos."[37]

Despite the focus of the Inquisitors, royal officials also acted to address Judaizing, owing perhaps to the much more extensive resources available to the Crown. The benefits to the Crown acting directly to punish Judaizing among Conversos were also tangible. Any fines would be directed to the royal coffers and not to those of the Inquisition. The initial action against Judaizing undertaken by royal officials occurred in 1393. In a surprising move, the officials swept the Jewish quarter on Passover where they rightly suspected that Judaizing Conversos would likely be celebrating Passover with their unbaptized Jewish family members. There were as noted previously, few Conversos in Morvedre, but the net nevertheless managed to catch a few perpetrators.

The Conversa Na Bella was fined 330 sous for having "had the pascha judahica with her one Jewish daughter." The Converso Pere Catala was fined 253 sous for having celebrated the Seder with his cousin.[38] Sol Avinacara and her baptized son were fined 1,650 Sous. The goal of the fines was to penalize Jews and Conversos sufficiently to deter future association.[39] The fines were apparently levied based on the financial assets of the individuals in question. In any case, the amounts were significant. Most important to note is that from the perspective of the families and presumably friends they shared Passover with, the Conversos present were Jews.[40]

The death of Queen Maria in 1406, removed a key impediment to the Inquisition's prosecution of Jews for assisting Conversos Judaize. For

---

[36] Ibid., 48- 49.

[37] Ibid., 50.

[38] Sous refers to coinage based on silver.

[39] Ibid., 38.

[40] Ibid., 186.

now, the Inquisition seemed content to penalize Jews financially. The charges had some merit as verified by the King's mention to his governor about the fines paid by many Jews. The King would not have allowed the inquisitors to penalize Jews by frivolous charges. The inquisitor, the bishop, and their followers were intent on applying severe pressure on Jews and Conversos.

In the city of Valencia, they disordered commercial activities with North Africa. They did so by accusing Jews, Conversos, and Muslim merchants of various undertakings and having them report to the bishop's court. They also vandalized the homes of Conversos they alleged were Judaizing. The activities of the Inquisition appear to have engendered or at least stirred already present emotions against Conversos among Old Christians. Some Old Christians began to call Conversos "circumcised dogs" along with other insults. As a consequence, some Conversos appear to have left the area and escaped to North Africa. [41]

In 1398, the inquisitional and papal officers whom King Marti allowed to run free found Conversos in the city of Morvedre still residing in the Jewish quarter, associating with their Jewish neighbors, and observing Jewish customs. [42] Mark Meyerson lays out the critical failures of the Crown as well as the Church in attempting to dissuade Conversos from continuing their Jewish practices and beliefs.

> "In the first decades after 1391, the most efficient way to putting a stop to the conversos' Judaizing and mingling with Jews would have been a thorough and systematic education of the converts in Catholic doctrine, the strict physical separation of Jews from conversos, and the full cooperation of the royal and ecclesiastical

---

[41] Ibid., 51-53.

[42] The relationship of Conversos and Jews could even exist when distance separated them. In Guadalupe, Starr-LeBeau notes that "A few New Christians had practicing Jewish family members at some distance, in southern Castile or in Muslim-controlled Malaga where New Christians were free to live as Jews. Guadalupense conversos occasionally traveled south to places like Seville, Alcocer, or Belacazar to visit with family or share briefly in a Jewish lifestyle. Catalina Rodriguez, the wife of Bartolome Rodriguez Narcies, had traveled to Seville to spend time in the Jewish quarter there before her family fled south permanently." Gretchen D. Starr-LeBeau, *In the Shadow of the Virgin: Inquisitors, Friars, and Conversos in Guadalupe, Spain* (Princeton, Princeton University Press, 2003), 92.

authorities in carrying out these tasks. The first was barely attempted; the second, owing to the Crown interest in fostering Jewish business, was pursued only halfheartedly; and the third was impeded by the inveterate, mutual mistrust of the Crown and Church. What indoctrination, segregation, and prosecution could not achieve, time eventually would, though only in part."[43]

The influence of Jews on Conversos continued throughout the 15th century. The Converso Martin Gutierrez, a clothing merchant from Guadalupe, learned about Jewish observances from visiting Jews. In 1485, one witness reported Gutierrez's activities to Inquisition. The witness Mari Sanchez noted that,

"...she heard Martin Gutierrez while standing at his door, ask a Jew who had come to buy goods how he kept the Sabbath. And the Jew said, 'Enter into your house, and I will tell you.' And Gutierrez called his children to hear what the Jew said and his children came, and the Jew said how the calf was prepared and other things that she does not remember."[44]

No practicing Jews lived in Guadalupe, but Martin Gutierrez took advantage of the exposure he had to live out a recognizable Jewish life.

---

[43] Ibid., 187-188.

[44] Gretchen D. Starr-LeBeau, *In the Shadow of the Virgin: Inquisitors, Friars, and Conversos in Guadalupe, Spain* (Princeton, Princeton University Press, 2003), 55.

CHAPTER 3

The Inquisition Reinvigorated

A papal Inquisition was in place in the Kingdom of Castile, but little activity had occurred. Political changes often involving Conversos drew attention to Judaizing. A seeming resurgence of Judaism in the 1460s in Castile initiated a new phase in the Christian polemic against both Jews and Conversos. The charges against Conversos were significant. Many of them circumcised their sons, observed Jewish rituals, and remained theologically Jewish.

To combat this pernicious heresy, the Franciscan preacher, writer, and later bishop, Fray Alonso de Espina, authored the work *Fortalitium Fidei* (The Fortress of Faith). His treatise sought to combat various heresies including Judaism. For De Espina, the solution was clear. Judaism had to be uprooted at its core to properly fight heresy among Conversos.

In 1459, in Segovia, he learned that the local Conversos had gone to the synagogue on the holiday of Succot. In 1459, in Fromista a Converso barber had boldly declared that he did not believe in Jesus, but rather in the God alone. The barber's declaration was reported to the bishop of the diocese of Palencia who, in turn, related it to Alfonso de Espina. The barber was originally sentenced to lifetime imprisonment, but his conviction was ultimately commuted to ten years' banishment from the town. De Espina charged inquisitors and the secular authorities to levy harsh penalties on Conversos who practiced circumcision.

Map of Medieval Iberian Kingdoms

On another occasion, De Espina spoke in the town of Medina del Campo against the heretics who pointed to errors in the New Testament. The heretics claimed it contained quotations from the prophets that were not found in the same usage as in the Hebrew Bible. De Espina argued that several Converso traders had heard a Converso monk make these statements while they visited Flanders. This had prompted them to undergo circumcision secretly when they returned to Medina del Campo. They were now about to set sail for North Africa while their associates were waiting for them in Seville.[1] According to De Espina, there were even those who practiced circumcision on the ground that Jesus had also been circumcised. If true, the melding of Jewish and Christian beliefs among Crypto-Jews was well underway.[2]

---

[1] Yitzhak Baer, *A History of the Jews in Christian Spain: Volume 2* (Philadelphia: Jewish Publication Society, 1961), 285-286.

[2] Starr-LeBeau writes that "While conversos in Guadalupe had some connection with Jews and even rabbis, maintaining a distinct theological tradition would have been difficult. New Christians attended mass and participated in other Christian rituals. As a result, it is likely that conversos absorbed Christian preoccupations with sin, atonement, and ultimate salvation to some degree. Gretchen D. Starr-LeBeau, *In the Shadow of the Virgin: Inquisitors, Friars, and Conversos in Guadalupe, Spain* (Princeton, Princeton University Press, 2003), 86.

De Espina preached in Medina del Campo in 1459 against Conversos practicing Jewish customs. Concurrent with his visit, thirty Conversos had purportedly just been circumcised and were secretly resting in the home of a friend during their recovery. De Espina claimed that one of them, a physician named Magister Franciscus, had even traveled to Jerusalem. Official records confirm this fact.[3]

On August 10th, 1461 he approached Alonso de Oropesa, the head of the Order of Saint Jerome, with this manuscript and plan.[4] Alonso de Oropesa defended Conversos on the basis that it was not just to suspect them simply because of their Jewish ancestry. He did, however, refer to Jews who were enticing Conversos and even old Christians to embrace Judaism in unforgiving terms.[5] Alonso de Oropesa argued that the medi-

---

[3] Yitzhak Baer notes that the official confirmation of Espina's claim regarding Magister Franciscus adds veracity to other stories related by him. He also adds that some other Conversos also intended to travel to Jerusalem. Ibid., 284-285. See the case of Converso from Morvedre who journeyed to Jerusalem. Mark D. Meyerson, *A Jewish Renaissance in Fifteenth-Century Spain* (Princeton: Princeton University Press, 2004), 201. Another case which supported De Espina's claims was that of Father Garcia Zapata. Zapata was the prior of the Hieronymite monastery. He celebrated the festival of Sukkot (Tabernacles) every September until his arrest and execution by the Inquisition tribunal in 1469. He was also accused of subsituting the proper words of consecration during the Eucharist with blasphemous phrases. This Inquisition operated under a local bishop. Joseph Perez, *The Spanish Inquisition: A History* (London: Profile Books, 2006), 17.

[4] Cecil Roth, *the Spanish Inquisition* (New York: W.W. Norton and Company, 1964), 40.

[5] Yitzhak Baer, *A History of the Jews in Christian Spain: Volume 2* (Philadelphia: Jewish Publication Society, 1961), 291. Starr –LeBeau notes the following: "When fray Alonso de Oropesa is remembered by scholars today, it is usually for taking up the converso standard against the Franciscans at court. However, Fray Alonso de Oropesa was not averse to the idea of an Inquisition; rather, he argued in his written works and in his statements at the court of Enrique IV for an Inquisition whose purpose would be to reform rather than to punish. Gretchen D. Starr-LeBeau, *In the Shadow of the Virgin: Inquisitors, Friars, and Conversos in Guadalupe, Spain* (Princeton, Princeton University Press, 2003), 115.

eval Inquisition, which had operated in the Kingdom of Aragon, should be similarly introduced into Castile.[6]

Alonso de Oropesa also agreed with Alonso de Espina that the very presence of Jews was an incitement to Conversos to Judaize.[7] The King acceded to Oropesa's request, but Alonso de Espina was not content. The medieval Inquisition had been inadequate in scope. In 1461, King Enrique IV petitioned Pope Pius II to establish an Inquisition in Castile. No response was given. The Pope died shortly after.[8] An episcopal inquisition was apparently held in Guadalupe in the 1460s, though its relation to Alonso de Espina's impetus is unclear. Fernando Gonzalez was a Converso who worked as a scribe for the Jeromite friary in the 1450s and 1460s. Gonzalez apparently revealed to some of the friars that he observed Jewish practices and was bold enough to speak disrespectfully of the Virgin Mary. Gonzalez's case is most interesting because of the involvement of Fray Diego de Marchena. Marchena knew of Gonzalez's practices but initially refused to disclose his identity when confronted by Prior Gonzalo de Madrid. Marchena was eventually accused of Judaizing. He was circumcised and under torture confessed that he had never been baptized.[9] He was found guilty and executed. Gonzalez was

---

[6] The first inquisitional investigation in Castile prior to the establishment of the Spanish Inquisition occurred in Guadalupe. This inquisition was active at the same time that Alonso de Oropesa was most active at the court of King Henry IV. It may have served as a more limited response to the Alonso de Espina's push for much more aggressive action. Gretchen D. Starr-LeBeau, *In the Shadow of the Virgin: Inquisitors, Friars, and Conversos in Guadalupe, Spain* (Princeton, Princeton University Press, 2003), 117.

[7] Joseph Perez, *History of a Tragedy: The Expulsion of the Jews from Spain* (Chicago: University of Illinois Press, 1993), 18.

[8] Norman Roth, "Anti-Converso Riots of the Fifteenth Century, Pulgar and the Inquisition," En la España medieval 15 (1992): 383.

[9] The toleration of Fray Diego de Marchena for some time may have been related to the fact that extensive financial support to the Jeronymites in Guadalupe was provided by the town's wealthiest Conversos. Conversos were also prominent in various town offices. The Conversos Diego Gonzalez and his son Andres Gonzalez de la Republica served as major and public defender respectively. Gretchen D. Starr-LeBeau, *In the Shadow of the Virgin: Inquisitors, Friars, and Conversos in Guadalupe, Spain* (Princeton, Princeton University Press, 2003), 121, 124.

initially penanced for his Judaizing but later executed for failing to complete his assigned penance.[10]

For De Spina, all Conversos were religiously suspect. His treatise lists twenty-five transgressions that Conversos committed.[11] Haim Beinart classifies the violations into three divisions. The first involved the observance of Jewish practices and beliefs. Among these are circumcision, the observance of the Sabbath, Jewish burial customs, the education of Converso children in synagogues, contributions of oil for synagogue lamps, taking Jewish oaths, and the expressions of belief in the Jewish faith.[12]

The second category included a broad range of actions committed against Christianity. These included evading the Sacraments, working on Sundays, avoiding mention of Jesus or Mary, slandering Mary and Christianity[13], eating lamb on Easter, attending Mass only for the purpose of throwing off suspicion to avoid excommunication[14],

---

[10] Gretchen D. Starr-LeBeau, *In the Shadow of the Virgin: Inquisitors, Friars, and Conversos in Guadalupe, Spain* (Princeton, Princeton University Press, 2003), 119-120.

[11] Haim Beinart, *Conversos on Trial: The Inquisition in Ciudad Real* (Jerusalem: The Magnes Press, 1981), 13.

[12] Ibid., 13. The Conversa Mari Sanchez gave oil to the synagogue in Trujillo and journeyed to visit the synagogue there. During her reconcilation to the Church, she was asked to name those who had entered the synagogue along with her. She included the name of an Old Christian. This may reveal that Judaism continued to be a curiosity even for sincere Christians. Gretchen D. Starr-LeBeau, *In the Shadow of the Virgin: Inquisitors, Friars, and Conversos in Guadalupe, Spain* (Princeton, Princeton University Press, 2003), 92, 154.

[13] Fray Alonso de Nogales believed that the Virgin Mary had conceived as other women had. He also questioned the doctrine of the annunication and the incarnation. Gretchen D. Starr-LeBeau, *In the Shadow of the Virgin: Inquisitors, Friars, and Conversos in Guadalupe, Spain* (Princeton, Princeton University Press, 2003), 210-211.

[14] Several Converso friars from Guadalupe, Fray Diego de Marchena and Fray Diego de Burgos were accused of improper behavior during Mass. Fray Alonso de Nogales of irreverance towards the Host. Fray Diego de Marchena also espoused the view that Jews and Muslims could be saved in their respective religions along with Christians. Gretchen D. Starr-LeBeau, *In the Shadow of the Virgin: Inquisitors, Friars, and Conversos in Guadalupe, Spain* (Princeton, Princeton University Press, 2003), 213, 215.

abstaining from making the sign of the cross, pretending that the lives of their babies were at danger at birth in order to prevent a formal church baptism, lending money at interest to Christians (as a means of atonement for their conversion to Christianity), false confessions, and theft or desecration of the Host.[15] Many of these elements are attested to by the earlier papal inquisitions operating in the kingdom of Aragon half a century earlier.

The final category included marriages among the various prohibited degrees of consanguinity. Alonso de Espina also accused Conversos of having abandoned belief in an afterlife.[16]

The Solution to the Conuerso Problem

Alonso de Espina maintained that faithful Christians had to avoid Conversos as much as possible. He rejected the proposition that integra-tion and assimilation would ultimately resolve the continued Jewish practices of Conversos. Segregation was the key to ensuring that faithful Christians were not dragged into heresy as well. The Cortes of Toledo adopted the policy of separation in 1480. Nevertheless, as the very Edict of Expulsion relates, the policy was ultimately a failure.[17]

De Spina argued that the Converso heresy should be dealt with by ac-tive investigation. The method for investigation was straightforward. Informers on individuals suspected of heresy were sought out. In short, as Beinart notes, de Espina called on every faithful Christian to seek out heretics. The actual examination of witnesses was to be done under the supervision of two members of the clergy, and ideally, a public notary would record their statements. As would be the case under the Inquis i-tion, a mere rumor of heresy was sufficient to initiate an investigation by archbishops, bishops, or archdeacons.

Suspects would be subject to examination at least once a year. If the accused confessed of their accord, then a light punishment sufficed to absolve the guilty party. If the accused did not confess within a year, he would be punished. The secular authorities handled carrying out pun-

---

[15] Haim Beinart, *Conversos on Trial: The Inquisition in Ciudad Real* (Jeru-salem: The Magnes Press, 1981), 13.

[16] Ibid.

[17] Ibid., 14.

ishment directed by the religious authorities. Their failure to do so would result in their dismissal. The inquisitors were also given the ability to act directly and arrest suspects themselves if warranted.[18]

De Spina stipulated that heretics would be excommunicated and divested of all ranks and honors. Excommunication applied to laymen, clerics, and public officials. Property owned by the accused was confiscated. The death penalty would be implemented as appropriate. Those heretics who abjured but later relapsed were to serve lifelong imprisonment.

Under De Spina's plan, descendants of heretics were barred from public office until the second generation. Anyone providing refuge to a heretic was to be excommunicated from the Church and ineligible for public office. They were also ineligible to serve as witnesses in court. Any Christian supporting Converso heretics and providing them with Christian burials would be excommunicated. They would not receive pardon unless they exhumed the corpse in question with their hands and discarded the bodies into a field.[19]

Alonso de Espina also sought to address the possibility of any favorable disposition towards Conversos. Any priest who urged a heretic to conceal his heresy was punished. Any bishop failing to impose adequately severe punishments would be removed from office for three

---

[18] Ibid., 15.

[19] Ibid., 16. The danger of ignoring the Converso problem is in the work *El Alboraique,* which relates words ascribed to St. Isidore of Seville. "Esta gente, si freno no les puiessen, sin rienda fuera a caer en mayors danos; pero darles-han una sofrenada e seguirse-ha la muerte de espada cruel en ellos, e cumplirse-a lo que dixo Moysen, Deuteronomio cap. Xxxii [...] 'oyd, cielos, el mi cuchillo cortara la carne', que quiere dezir: 'dara venganza a mis apasionadores e a mis malquerientes dare mal galardon. 'E Sant Ysidoro dize, levantarse-ha una heregia en Espana de las gentes que crucifaron a Christo, e durara setenta anos, y al cabo del ano de senteta sera destruydos por fuego y espada.'" "These people, if they are not stopped, without reigns they will fall into terrible danger...and St. Isidore said a great heresy in Spain has emerged from those who crucified Christ and it will last for seventy years. At the end of the seventy years it will end in fire and sword." Prologo 403 cited in Jeremy Lawrance, "Alegoria Y Apocalipsis En El Alboraique," Revista de Poetica Medieval, 11 (2009): 34.

years. Lower rank clergy were to be excommunicated and were to be granted pardon by the Pope alone or on their death bed.[20]

Alonso de Espina regarded the forced baptism of children as acceptable even if their parents protested. Expulsion proved to be the only real remedy for obstinate Jews as far as De Espina was concerned.[21] His proposal enjoyed some success with the establishment of inquisitional tribunals in the ecclesiastical courts of Toledo and Castilian localities. By the following decade, however, his views were adopted by those spearheading the charge against Converso integration in Spanish society.[22]

The Inquisition Unleashed

Seville's Jewish population suffered the first onslaught in 1391 and never recovered as a center of Jewish life. The city had nevertheless, seen an enlarged community of Conversos who took advantage of the commercial prospects available in this thriving seaport. By 1480, up to eight thousand Conversos may have resided in the city, which may mean that Conversos represented up to twenty percent of Seville's population. When the Inquisitional tribunal was set up in Seville, many Conversos fled to the territories of considerate nobles such as Rodrigo Ponce de Leon, Marquis of Cádiz, Enrique de Guzman, Duke of Medina Sidonia, and Pedro Puertocarrero, the Count of Palma.[23]

---

[20] Haim Beinart, *Conversos on Trial: The Inquisition in Ciudad Real* (Jerusalem: The Magnes Press, 1981), 18.

[21] Ibid., 20.

[22] Ibid.

[23] Cecil Roth, *The Spanish Inquisition* (New York: W.W. Norton and Company, 1964), 47.

Saint Dominic Guzman Presiding an Auto de Fé by Pedro Berruguette

The Inquisitors quickly addressed the attempt to escape its jurisdiction. On January 2, 1481, the inquisitors issued an edict to Rodrigo Ponce de Leon, the Marquis of Cadiz, and to all dukes, counts, grand masters of military orders, and knights in the area. They also issued it to the mayors of Seville, Córdoba, Jerez de la Frontera, Toledo, and various others in Castile. They were ordered to arrest any absconding Conversos which had taken refuge among them. They were also sentenced to confiscate their property. If they failed to do so, they were subject to arrest themselves.

Anyone refusing to obey this proclamation was subject to excommunication and forfeiture of their property, public offices, and titles. While the numbers are difficult to verify, the region under the stewardship of the Marquis of Cadiz was reported to have turned away 8,000 Conversos.[24] They were returned to Seville and delivered to the Inquisition for processing. Wealth and status did not offer any protection to Conversos accused of Judaizing. The tribunal in Seville was eventually transferred to the castle of Triana near Seville.

---

[24] Ibid., 47.

The first *auto da fé* in Seville was held on February 6, 1481. Six men and women were burned.[25] Alfonso de Hojeda preached at this *auto da fé* but fell victim to an epidemic which was then spreading in Andalusia. Within a few days, three of the most important Conversos of Seville, among them the previously mentioned conspirator Diego de Susán who was designated as a rabbi, Manuel Sauli, and Bartolome de Torralba were executed. Others caught from the conspiracy to fight the Inquisitors were also burned.

These included Fernandez Benadeva, Pedro Fernandez Cansino, and Gabriel de Zamora. The latter two were municipal councilors of Seville. Abulafia the Perfumed, Medina el Barbudo the meat commissary at Seville, the municipal councilor Pedro de Jaen and his son Juan del Monte were also included among the victims. Other fatalities included Aleman Poca Sangre, the Aldafes brothers, Alvaro de Sepulveda the Elder and his son Juan de Xerez. The wealth of those arrested was significant and by Inquisitional policy seized by the royal treasury.[26]

The number of casualties becomes problematic to quantify. It appears that Seville held at least one *auto da fé* every month for some duration. On the *auto da fé* held on March 26, 1481, 17 Conversos were burned with more following a few weeks later. Another 298 Conversos were executed, with a further 98 condemned to life imprisonment by November.[27] The Inquisition also held trials in Córdoba and the archbishopric

---

[25] Ibid., 45.

[26] Singer, Isidore; Adler, Cyrus; (eds.) The Jewish Encyclopedia, "Inquisition: called also Sanctum Officium or Holy Office." Last modified 1904. Accessed January 2, 2013. goo.gl/SX6f8D

[27] Cecil Roth, *The Spanish Inquisition* (New York: W.W. Norton and Company, 1964), 48. Joseph Perez notes the discrepancy between the authorization date for the Inquisition in Castile given on November 1, 1478 and the two year delay of its implementation. According to Perez, the delay was possibly due to Queen Isabella's reticence to activate an institution that would violently repress Judaizing. Joseph Perez, *The Spanish Inquisition: A History* (London: Profile Books, 2006), 20. Cardinal Pedro Gonzalez de Mendoza originally supported the establishment of the Inquisition, but sought to win Conversos "back" to the Church by instruction. He authored the work titled Catecismo de la doctrina Cristiana and hoped to instruct Conversos. Salo Wittmayer Baron, *A Social and the Religious History of the Jews: Volume XIII* (Philadelphia: Jewish Publication Society, 1969), 27.

of Cadiz. Some Judaizers were burned under these tribunals the same year. 700 executions between 1481 and 1488 are commonly asserted.[28]

The Inquisition offered a period of reprieve for Conversos who were guilty of observing Jewish customs if they appeared voluntarily before the court and confessed their sins. The pardon granted those who were considered truly repentant. A guarantee of their property rights and freedom was promised.[29] Many Conversos took advantage of this offer, but the conditions for absolution were altered to include the following requirements.

Penitent Conversos were expected to divulge the names, professions, residences, and practices of persons they knew to be Judaizers or had heard to be. Once the decree expired, anyone whose name had been provided was summoned to appear before the tribunal in three days. Inquisitional authorities arrested those who failed to attend. A statement was issued revealing Judaizing practices.

"If they celebrate the Sabbath, wear a clean shirt or better garments, spread a clean tablecloth, light no fire, eat the food which has been cooked overnight in the oven, or perform no work on that day; if they eat meat during Lent; if they take neither meat nor drink on the Day of Atonement, go barefoot, or ask forgiveness of another on that day; if they celebrate the Passover with unleavened bread, or eat bitter herbs; if on the Feast of Tabernacles they use green branches or send fruit as gifts to friends; if they marry according to Jewish customs or take Jewish names; if they circumcise their boys or observe the 'hadas', that is, celebrate the seventh night after the birth of a child by filling a vessel with water, throwing in gold, silver, pearls, and grain, and then bathing the child while certain prayers are recited; if they throw a piece of dough in the stove before baking; if they wash their hands before praying, bless a cup of wine before meals and pass it round among the people at table; if they pronounce blessings while slaughtering poultry, cover the

---

[28] Joseph Perez, *The Spanish Inquisition: A History* (London: Profile Books, 2006), 27. See also Yitzhak Baer, *A History of the Jews in Christian Spain: Volume 2* (Philadelphia: Jewish Publication Society, 1961), 327.

[29] Cecil Roth, *The Spanish Inquisition* (New York: W.W. Norton and Company, 1964), 48.

blood with earth, separate the veins from meat, soak the flesh in water before cooking, and cleanse it from blood; if they eat no pork, hare, rabbits, or eels; if, soon after baptizing a child, they wash with water the spot touched by the oil; give Old Testament names to their children, or bless the children by the laying on of hands; if the women do not attend church within forty days after confinement; if the dying turn toward the wall; if they wash a corpse with warm water; if they recite the Psalms without adding at the end: 'Glory be to the Father, the Son, and the Holy Ghost, etc.'"[30]

Seville faced a severe financial situation as a consequence of having lost a crucial source of income with the departure of so many Conversos. It also came about because the agents, who collected the taxes, were themselves Conversos and possibly fled as well. The economic situation was so dangerous that the crown presented Conversos. In exchange for a financial inducement, a family could eliminate the blemish of a sentence from the Inquisition's archives. Many wealthier Conversos accepted the offer and started to return to the city.[31]

Pope Sixtus IV by Tiziano Vicelli

---

[30] Singer, Isidore; Adler, Cyrus; (eds.) The Jewish Encyclopedia, "Inquisition: called also Sanctum Officium or Holy Office." Last modified 1904. Accessed January 2, 2013. https://goo.gl/SX6f8D

[31] Kevin Ingram, "Secret lives, public lies: the conversos and socio-religious non-conformism in the Spanish Golden Age." (PhD diss., UC San Diego, 2006), http://escholarship.org/uc/item/6270j25z. 143-144.

From Seville, inquisitors were sent to the towns of Córdoba, Jaen, Ciudad Real, and possibly to Segovia to track any Converso fugitives. They were also empowered to appropriate their property. However, the harsh tactics employed by the inquisitors at Seville raised concern even in Rome. Complaints made to Sixtus IV were addressed in a letter written on January 29, 1482, to King Ferdinand and Queen Isabella.

The letter amended the bull of November 1, 1478, and related his displeasure. Pope Sixtus IV had apparently envisioned an organization along the lines of the Medieval Inquisition. The Pope's castigation was largely empty. While he reprimanded the inquisitors, Miguel de Morillo and Juan de San Martin remained in their posts. While he did initially refuse to appoint inquisitors for the other areas requested by King Ferdinand and Queen Isabella, two weeks later on February 11, 1482, he appointed Vicar-General Alfonso de San Capriani inquisitor-general for the kingdoms of Castile and Leon. Seven other members of the clergy including Tomas de Torquemada were installed as inquisitors.

The tension continued, however as King Ferdinand attempted to establish his Inquisitors in Valencia and Saragossa in December 29th, 1481. The Pope was incensed and suspended inquisitional activities in the Kingdom of Aragon on April 18th, 1482. The impasse continued until October 17th, 1483. The Pope finally relented and agreed to appoint Tomas de Torquemada as chief inquisitor of Aragon.[32] Earlier that year, the Inquisition ordered that all Jews leave the archbishopric of Seville and the bishopric of Cordoba.[33]

[32] Joseph Perez, *The Spanish Inquisition: A History* (London: Profile Books, 2006), 31.

[33] Yitzhak Baer, *A History of the Jews in Christian Spain: Volume 2* (Philadelphia: Jewish Publication Society, 1961), 330.

In a letter which partly buttresses the arguments of scholars such as Benzion Netanyahu, the Pope while recognizing Queen Isabella's piety, referenced his concern over "ambition and greed for earthly possessions, rather than by zeal for the faith and true fear of God." Despite the mild reproof, the pope granted some concessions. While reiterating in his bull of May 25, 1483, that the pope was the only power to whom final appeal could be made in matters of faith, at the request of King Ferdinand and Queen Isabella, he appointed the Archbishop of Seville, Inigo Manrique, appellate court judge for Spain. The Pope also decreed that all officials of the Inquisition be required to be of pure Christian descent and in no degree related to Conversos. The Pope, however, did issue another bull titled Ad Futuram Rei Memoriam on August 2 in which he ordered any repentant Conversos from Rome who had completed their penance was no longer to be persecuted by the Inquisition.

The population count of 1494 noted 2,000 Conversos listed out of a total number of inhabitants of 40,000. The census, however, had taken place after fourteen years of Inquisitional action. During this period, hundreds if not thousands of Conversos were burned. Several thousand Conversos also fled the city in the wake of the tribunal's activities. The chroniclers Andres Bernaldez and Hernando de Pulgar also notes that another 3,000 Converso families escaped to Portugal, France, and North Africa where many of them returned to Judaism. Despite the catastrophe that the Converso population of Seville would see, by the first decades of the sixteenth century, the Converso community of Seville improved its fortunes. Some prosperous Converso merchants were able to purchase positions for their kinfolk on the town council as well as in the Cathedral. From this place of prominence, they were able to participate importantly in local matters.[34]

The Appointment of Thomas de Torquemada

On October 17, 1483, Thomas de Torquemada was appointed inquisitor-general. His principal concern was making the Inquisition more efficient in its reach. Tribunals were quickly established in Córdoba,

---

[34] Ibid., 145.

Jaen, and Ciudad Real.[35] In Córdoba, the first inquisitors to be appointed were Pedro Martinez de Barrio and Alvar Gonzalez. Among the first victims of the tribunal was Pedro Fernandez de Alcaudete, treasurer of a church.[36] In Jaen, the first inquisitors appointed were Juan Garcia de Canas, chaplain to the King and Queen, and Juan de Yarca. In Ciudad Real, the first inquisitors appointed were Pedro Diaz de Costana and Francisco Sanchez de la Fuente. In Ciudad Real, the Inquisition operated for only two years. From February 6, 1484, to May 6, 1485, ten *autos da fé* were held there. The largest was celebrated on February 23-24, 1484, and March 15, 1485. In Ciudad Real, one Converso functioned as a ritual slaughterer, and another served as the "rabbi" for other Conversos.[37]

On February 23 approximately 34 Conversos were condemned to execution.[38] These included Alvaro de Belmonte, Pero Çarça, Maestre Fernando, and Maria Gonsales la Pampana. Juan Gonsales Pampana, the husband of the aforesaid Maria Gonsales, was burned in effigy on the following day. Another 41 individuals had fled.[39] On March 15, 1485, another 8 people were burned with another 54 burned in effigy. One of the victims, Juan Gonsales Escogid, was characterized as a rabbi and "Confesor de los Confesos." In May 1485, the tribunal of Ciudad Real completed its activity and was transferred to Toledo.

Torquemada authored an inquisitorial constitution initially containing twenty-eight articles. It included a reprieve of thirty or forty days for those accused of Judaizing. Those who voluntarily confessed within this time could on payment of a small fine and further contributions to the state treasury preserve their property. The penitents were to make their confession in writing before the inquisitors and several witnesses to qualify for this reprieve. In most cases, a public recantation would follow. Those individuals confessing after the expiration of the respite

---

[35] Cecil Roth, *The Spanish Inquisition* (New York: W.W. Norton and Company, 1964), 49. See also See also Jean Plaidy, *The Spanish Inquisition: Its Rise, Growth, and End* (New York:, Barnes and Nobles, 1994), 123-133.

[36] Adolfo de Castro, *Judios en España* (Cadiz: Revista Medica, 1847), 118.

[37] Yitzhak Baer, *A History of the Jews in Christian Spain: Volume 2* (Philadelphia: Jewish Publication Society, 1961), 336.

[38] Ibid., 334.

[39] See Singer, Isidore; Adler, Cyrus; (eds.) The Jewish Encyclopedia, "Inquisition: called also Sanctum Officium or Holy Office." Last modified 1904. Accessed January 2, 2013. goo.gl/SX6f8D

were punished by having their property confiscated or by imprisonment for life depending on the severity of the offense. The tribunal also de-creed special treatment of Conversos under the age of under twenty years of age who claimed that they were forced by their parents or other persons to observe Jewish practices. These individuals were not subject to confiscation of their property. Nevertheless, they were obliged to wear the sanbenito for a certain length of time.

Convicted Heretic with Sanbenito and coroza by Francisco de Goya

The offer of amnesty was applied in other cities as well. One example is the case of Juan Sánchez de Cepeda. In 1485, this wealthy Toledo silk merchant and the paternal grandfather of Teresa of Avila admitted to the newly established Inquisition tribunal that he had committed "many grave crimes and offenses" against the Catholic Church. This confession was made during the Inquisition's forty day period of grace, in which Conversos were encouraged to admit their apostasy to receive light sentences.[40]

---

[40] Confessing during the period of grace did not guarantee escape from pun-ishment. Starr-Lebeau notes "For the inquisitors, statements of reconcilation were almost expected from local conversos and were seen as a sign of guilt ra-ther than repentance. They served as an introduction to the paradoxical world of the inquisistor; where coercion made possible, the profoundly tainted, all communication between the Court and the accused." Gretchen D. Starr-LeBeau,

During this time 2,400 Conversos, (15 percent of the city's total population of Old and New Christians), presented themselves to the Inquisitors for sentencing. It is theoretically possible that not all these people were, in fact, Judaizers. They were, however, members of a minority group that lived in its neighborhoods, formed endogamous marriages and business unions and maintained discrete cultural practices (bathing on the Sabbath, refraining from eating pork products, etc.), and this visible social non-conformity made them potential targets. Once they confessed, they were branded forever. Apparently, the majority of Toledo's Conversos believed that it was wiser to genuflect before the Holy Office in this period of amnesty, rather than await a next attack that would carry far greater consequences. What they did not realize, however, was that in volunteering information on their Jewish backgrounds they were presenting the Holy Office with relevant data that it would use against them and their families in the future.[41]

Accused individuals confessing after the reprieve, but before sentencing was pronounced were to undergo the progress of "reconciliation" which saved them from a death sentence. Despite their confession, they were potentially subject to life imprisonment. Anyone failing to disclose their sins was condemned to death. If a suspected Conversos would not confess, then torture was authorized.

If however, they recanted their confession or their testimony was suspect, then they were once again to undergo torture. The sentencing options available to the Inquisition included incarceration for the short term or life imprisonment. It also included death by fire. If the condemned were to be executed, they were tied to the stake and burned alive. If however, the convicted confessed before death, then as an act of mercy the prisoner would be strangled before the pyre was lit. Anyone that was accused but had fled was deemed guilty of the defendant's

---

In the Shadow of the Virgin: Inquisitors, Friars, and Conversos in Guadalupe, Spain (Princeton, Princeton University Press, 2003), 154.

[41] Kevin Ingram, "Secret lives, public lies: the conversos and socio-religious non-conformism in the Spanish Golden Age." (PhD diss., UC San Diego, 2006), 164-165.

crimes and regarded as a relapse to Judaism. The property of the escapee was seized they were burned in effigy.[42]

The Inquisition in Aragon, Catalonia, and Valencia

Under the direction of Torquemada, the Inquisition was established in the region of Catalonia on October 17, 1483.[43] In the case of Valencia, the papal Inquisition had operated there since 1420, and Episcopal inquisitors had conducted in the general vicinity shortly after the mass conversions of 1391. The then current inquisitor was the Dominican Juan Cristobal de Gualbes but was replaced by Pedro d'Epila and Martin Iñigo. In Aragon, the papal inquisition had also been active, but to transform it under the current administration required the consent of the Cortes. After extensive debate in the Cortes, permission was granted on April 1484. Gaspar Juglar and Pedro Arbues, the canon of the metropolitan church of Saragossa were selected as inquisitors of Aragon. Saragossa saw its first tribunals on May 10, 1484, under the oversight of Maestre Julian. Conversos eventually poisoned him.[44]

The Death of the Inquisitor Pedro Arbues

Violent resistance met the Inquisition's introduction and reorganization in Aragon and the region of Catalonia in certain quarters. Conversos and their descendants considered the Inquisition as a serious threat. Faced with this opposition, the Cortes determined to send a delegation to the King to protest to the Inquisition. With the King resolute in his resistance to Converso attempts to mitigate the Inquisition's power, some conspired to assassinate the Inquisitor Pedro Arbues.[45] Gaspar Ju-

---

[42] Singer, Isidore; Adler, Cyrus; (eds.) The Jewish Encyclopedia, "Inquisition: called also Sanctum Officium or Holy Office." Last modified 1904. Accessed January 2, 2013. goo.gl/SX6f8D

[43] Cecil Roth, *The Spanish Inquisition* (New York: W.W. Norton and Company, 1964), 51.

[44] Ibid., 53.

[45] Toby Green, *Inquisition: The Reign of Fear* (New York: St. Martin's Press, 2007), 20-21.

glar died in January 1485. He was rumored to have been poisoned by Conversos, but no evidence exists to confirm this.[46]

Any hope of impeding the Inquisition's work was quickly dispelled, however. Once Arbues' murder was discovered the old Christian population reacted in violent anger and proceeded to attack the aljama where Jews as well as many Conversos continued to reside.[47] A massacre was averted only through the intervention of the Archbishop Alfonso de Aragon who placated the masses. The assassination of Arbues prompted a strong reaction by Inquisitional authorities that had a long term impact for years. Beginning on December 15, 1485, and continuing through the beginning of the sixteenth century, the Inquisition held approximately one or two *autos da fé* nearly every month in Saragossa.

The Death of Pedro Arbues by Francesco Cecchini

From 1485 through 1500, more than fifty *autos da fé* were held at Saragossa. In 1492 alone, nine took place. The punishment on members of the conspiracy is especially severe. Juan de Esperanden had his hands

---

[46] Joseph Perez, *The Spanish Inquisition: A History* (London: Profile Books, 2006), 33.

[47] Cecil Roth, *The Spanish Inquisition* (New York: W.W. Norton and Company, 1964), 54.

cut off. He was then dragged along with another fellow conspirator, Vidal de Urango to the market where both were beheaded. Their punishment continued with their bodies being quartered and lastly burned on June 30, 1486. On December 15 Francisco de Sante Fé was also executed despite the high estimation in which the governor of Aragon held him. Juan de la Abadia was dragged through the streets, quartered, and burned on January 21, 1487. A few weeks later, the following the Jesuit Juan Martinez de Rueden was also burned, anti-Christian books in Hebrew having been found in his possession.[48] His relative, the widow of Antonio de Rueda of Catalayud, was also burned on April 10, 1492. She was found guilty of observing the Sabbath and of regularly eating Jewish hamin. Gaspar de S. Cruce and Juan Pedro Sanchez escaped to the city of Toulouse but were nevertheless burned in effigy.[49]

Opposition to the Inquisition in Toledo

The opposition levied against the Inquisition by Conversos in Saragossa was also repeated by Conversos in Toledo. The inquisitors Pero Diaz de la Costana and Vasco Ramirez de Ribera entered Toledo on May 1485. By June 2 Conversos attacked one of them. The attack proved unsuccessful, and the conspirators captured the Converso, De la Torre and four of his cohorts were strangled and hanged.

---

[48] Some Conversos obtained books that helped them determine the dates for Jewish holidays and how to observe Jewish law. Juana Gonzalez from Guadalupe was arrested by the Inquistion and confessed that "her husband Lope de Herrera had a book of the law of Moses in which was written all the feasts and holidays and fasts for the whole year based on the law, and how do them and in what manner, and there were prayers in the said law of Moses." The number of Jewish books owned by Conversos in Guadalupe was so significant that the Inquisitors burned two trunks filled with them at one *auto de fé*. Gretchen D. Starr-LeBeau, *In the Shadow of the Virgin: Inquisitors, Friars, and Conversos in Guadalupe, Spain* (Princeton, Princeton University Press, 2003), 84-85.

[49] Henry C. Lea, "The Martyrdom of S. Pedro Arbues," Papers of the American Historical Society (1889): During this period, hundreds of members of the most prominent Conversos families including members of those of Sanchez, Caballeria, Santangel, Paternoy, Monfort, Ram, Almaçan, and Clemente were either burned or sentenced to life imprisonment.

A Condemned Heretic Wearing a Sambenito

In a move that reverberated throughout the community, the Inquisitors summoned the local rabbi, and demanded under oath and on pain of severe punishment, that they threaten excommunication on any Jew who knew of Conversos observing Jewish practices and failed to report this to the Inquisition. Some Jews informed on Conversos out of concern, while others purportedly did so out of spite, perhaps because of the success which many Conversos had achieved. At least eight of these witnesses were tortured at the command of Queen Isabella after the veracity of their testimony was called into question.[50]

The first *auto da fé* in Toledo took place on February 12, 1486. Approximately 750 persons were received back into the Church with another 1,650 individuals by June 11th. Not all Conversos were so fortunate. On August 16 of the same year, for example, 25 people, including Alfonso Cota were burned. On August 17 the pastor of Talavera and a cleric, both of whom were found guilty of observing Judaism were executed. On October 15 several hundred deceased individuals were burned in effigy and their property confiscated by the state. On December 10, 950 persons received absolution. By March 10, 1487, an addi-

---

[50] Singer, Isidore; Adler, Cyrus; (eds.) The Jewish Encyclopedia, "Inquisition: called also Sanctum Officium or Holy Office." Last modified 1904. Accessed January 2, 2013. goo.gl/SX6f8D

tional 1,900 Judaizers were readmitted to the Church after confessing their sins.

On May 7 however, 23 individuals, including a canon, were executed. They were joined on July 25, 1488, by an additional 37 persons. Two days later 6 clericals accused of Judaizing were also burned. On May 24, 1490, another 21 people were also burned at the stake while 11 others were sentenced to life imprisonment. On the next day, the bones of 400 corpses designated as Judaizers were collected along with a collection of Hebrew books.[51] They formed a pyre for a woman whom the Inquisition had sentenced to death and rather than accept the garrote who wished to die as a professing Jewess. On July 25, 1492, only eight days before the expulsion, 5 Conversos were burned at the stake while others were sentenced to life imprisonment. On July 30, 1494, 16 people from the cities of Guadalajara, Alcalá de Henares, and Toledo were burned. An additional 30 were sentenced to life imprisonment. In 1496, another three *autos da fé* were held with another two held the following year.[52]

By the end of the fifteenth century, almost a dozen tribunals had been established in Spain. One court was set in the city of Guadalupe in the province of Estremadura. The inquisitor, Nuno de Arevato, proceeded

---

[51] Salo Wittmayer Baron, *A Social and the Religious History of the Jews: Volume XIII* (Philadelphia: Jewish Publication Society, 1969), 32. The previously mentioned Converso Martin Gutierrez owned a Jewish prayer book. Juan de Cabeza reported that Gutierrez would "pray each morning from a book, behind the door, and bowing; and although he asked him what he should do he did not respond until he had finshed praying." Miguel Sanchez Zohano also appeared as a witness to the Inquisition. The following was recorded: "Eight or nine years ago this witness entered the house of Martin Gutierrez one morning...he entered and called out, and the said Martin Gutierrez did not hear him, and he was among some chests lying face down with a hood on his head and he was bowing and praying; and this witness did not understand what he prayed but it did not seem like Christian prayers;...And this witness left the house and banged loudly on the door, and then the said Martin Gutierrez got up and threw off the hood that he had on his head." Gretchen D. Starr-LeBeau, *In the Shadow of the Virgin: Inquisitors, Friars, and Conversos in Guadalupe, Spain* (Princeton, Princeton University Press, 2003), 59.

[52] Singer, Isidore; Adler, Cyrus; (eds.) The Jewish Encyclopedia, "Inquisition: called also Sanctum Officium or Holy Office." Last modified 1904. Accessed January 2, 2013. goo.gl/SX6f8D

meticulously against Conversos living there. While the tribunal existed for only a few years, seven *autos da fé* were held beginning in 1485. 52 Conversos accused of Judaizing were executed. A further 25 were condemned in absentia and burned in effigy. These images were burned together with the bones of 46 corpses. A further 16 were sentenced to life imprisonment. Others were condemned to wear the sanbenito, and deprived of their property.

Opposition to the Inquisition in Catalonia

In Catalonia, the Inquisition also met substantial resistance. In 1486 riots broke out at Teruel, Lerida, Barcelona, and Valencia which saw the newly introduced tribunals destroyed. In 1487, Inquisitor-general Torquemada appointed Alfonso de Espina of Huesca inquisitor of Barcelona. On January 25, 1488, De Espina held an *auto da fé*. The first victim was a royal official who was a descendant of a renowned self-loathing Jew, Geronimo de Santa Fé.

Some other prominent individuals eventually fell victim to the Inquisition in Catalonia. On May 2, 1489, for example, the wife of Jacob Monfort, the former Catalonian treasurer, was burned in effigy. On March 5 and 23, 1490, Louis Ribelles, a physician from Falces, along with his children and daughter-in-law was sentenced to life imprisonment. His wife Constancia fell victim only a few days later and was burned on March 12 in Tarracona. On March 24, 1490, several prominent individuals, Gabriel Miro and his wife Blanquina, Gaspar de la Cavalleria and his wife were burned in effigy. Simon de Santangel and his wife were denounced to the Inquisition at Huesca as Judaizers by their son and were burned on July 30, 1490, in Lerida.

Jews Involved in Inquisitions Proceedings

The Inquisition required local rabbis to issue a synagogue ban on any Jew failing to reveal facts on Christian heretics or relapsed converts.[53] In Teruel for example, it forced Rabbi Simuel to testify on July 25th, 1485. His testimony appears to have been limited to many Conversos who

---

[53] Salo Wittmayer Baron, *A Social and the Religious History of the Jews: Volume XIII* (Philadelphia: Jewish Publication Society, 1969), 37.

were already deceased. Another witness related the Converso families who observed the Day of Atonement and other Jewish practices. The witness described what his daughter had seen while serving as a servant in some of the Converso homes. The witness added that "...all the other confesos [conversos], though bearing the name of Christians, are nothing but pure Jews in their practices and conversations."[54]

In the region of Catalonia, Inquisitional activity was largely restricted to a small number of *autos da fé*. The number of victims was consequently limited. The Inquisition in Castile, however, was much more active. On June 19, 1488, the tribunal of Valladolid held its first *auto da fé*. 18 persons who had openly confessed Jewish practices were sentenced to death.

The first inquisitors in the city of Segovia were Dr. de Mora and the licentiate De Caña. The first individual to be condemned to the stake was Gonzalo de Cuellar. The royal treasury confiscated his substantial property by standard Inquisitional practice. The involvement of unconverted Jews in the indictment against Gonzalo is surprising. Drawn into the process against him were his Jewish relatives. These included Don Moses de Cuellar, his sons Rabbi Abraham and his brother, and Juan Chalfon Conbiador and Isaac Herrera from Segovia.[55] From 1490 until the end of the 15th century over 100 persons were condemned to the stake in Avila for Judaizing. 70 others received various degrees of punishment.

Music as Evidence of Judaizing

The Spanish Inquisition was focused on a wide array of markers which may have indicated Judaizing among Conversos. The basic list compiled by Elias Lindo has already been reviewed. Even something as seemingly innocuous music was cause for suspicion, however. In May 1489, Rabbi Simuel, the doctor to the Duke of Albuquerque, testified under oath that he had heard his father speak about a certain Diego Ari-

---

[54] Ibid., 29.

[55] At Avila the first victims were the Francos, who were accused of having murdered the child La Guardia referenced in Singer, Isidore; Adler, Cyrus; (eds.) The Jewish Encyclopedia, "Inquisition: called also Sanctum Officium or Holy Office." Last modified 1904. Accessed January 2, 2013. goo.gl/SX6f8D

as' musical tastes. Diego Arias had apparently sung it to Rabbi Simucl's father while the two were alone. In April 1486, another rabbi, David Gome had also testified that he heard a certain Jacob mention Diego Arias' signing.[56]

In this particular case, the incidence had occurred at a lodge in Medi-na del Campo. The Jacob in question, Jacob Castellano, a Jewish resident of the town related that around 1460, Diego Arias had associated with Jews. Another rabbi, Mosses aben Mayor also testified that he had heard Yuce Aben Major discuss Arias' singing. The issue was that Diego Arias was singing Jewish songs while he traveled, in Jewish households, in the privacy of his home, and in various other locations. Another witness stated that Diego Arias said,

> "If there was anything after this world for the soul…it was the voices of the prayers of the Jews which would do for him because behind the said monastery of La Merced there was a synagogue."[57]

Gutwirth states: "Music was not seen as divorced from the spaces of religious identity." Gurwirth notes the extent of the relationships that Diego Arias maintained with Jews. Jacob Castellano was an official of the Jewish community; the others were rabbis and forced part of Diego Arias circle.[58] On the importance of language as a characteristic of identity, Gutwirth states the following:

> "One on occasion, for example, we are told that Diego Arias asked a Jew 'whether he knew how to sing something in his Hebrew, and he answered that he did. Music is here not only a question of knowledge, 'si sabia,' but also of ethnicity, 'su hebrayco,' where the possessive pronoun indicates the converso's perception of the Jews' possession of Hebrew language, poetic texts, and songs."[59]

---

[56] Eleazar Gutwirth, "Music, Identity, and the Inquisition in Fifteenth-Century Spain," Early Music History, Vol. 17 (1998): 165.

[57] Ibid., 166.

[58] Ibid., 167-168.

[59] Ibid., 169-170.

CHAPTER 4

The Edicts of Expulsion

Unconverted Jews were accused of undermining the Christian faith of Conversos by reinforcing their knowledge of Jewish practices and beliefs. The Edict of Expulsion lists this as the chief motive, and there is no reason to doubt that the religious concern of King Ferdinand and Queen Isabella was a legitimate one from their standpoint.

The idea that some Jews missionized or proselytized Conversos was based on fact. Sometime in the 1450s in Morvedre, one of the Adzonis brothers worked to convince the Converso Pere de la Rosa that the Torah of Moses was the real law. Salvation argued Adzoni was achieved by performing Jewish observances. Other Conversos such as Joan Aldomar and Jaume Scriva who were already convinced as to the virtue of Judaism provided Pere with additional reinforcement. Another example is provided by the testimony of Fray Alonso de Plasencia. Fray Alonso recalled a conversation of Fray Diego de Marchena with a man from Durango.

"...speaking with Marchena, with the man from Durango, and with Fray Estevan, the man from Durango said, 'Something has happened in this town that has not happened in all Castile.' And the man from Marchena said, ' I will tell you what it is.' Two rabbis have been walking all through Castile, visiting [Conversos to see] if the Law of Moses was being observed properly, and they came to this town and asked if they kept the law of Moses. And some said yes, and others said that they could not keep it well because they were poor. And [the rabbis] granted them a dispensation so that they could work on the holidays, and these were the poor shoemakers and other poor people."[1]

The persuasion of Conversos appears to have often been a cooperative effort between Conversos and Jews. Elionor Canella was also convinced to return to Judaism by a Jew named Civello, but Civello's arguments were also supported by Ursula Forcadell, a Judaizing Conversa. The crux of the argument given to Elionor was as follows: "a Jew induced her to believe in the Law of Moses, telling her that it is the only law and that she should not believe that there is a Trinity but [should believe] that there is only one God who created the heavens, stars, sea, and sands."[2] Convinced by Civello and Forcadell, Elionor and her husband also a Converso, attended a Passover Seder at Ursula Forcadell's home. They also observed Yom Kippur when Morvedre inducted a new rabbi.

Other Jews in the area of Morvedre were also active in teaching Conversos. A bearded Jew read the Converso Bernat Guimera a Hebrew parchment. A rabbi named Abraham instructed the children of Joan Frances to read and write Hebrew at the request of their father.[3] Violant Natera exemplifies the degree to which continuing relationships between Jews and Conversos were common in 1509. Arrested by the Inquisition, Natera revealed the following to her fellow inmate:

"Many Jews used to come to the house of her mother; they taught many things. Once there came a Jew very learned in that law; it was a marvel to hear the things he said and knew about the law. And he gave amulets to her and her sisters. And that Jew and her mother debated about that law, and it was a blessing to

---

[1] Gretchen D. Starr-LeBeau, *In the Shadow of the Virgin: Inquisitors, Friars, and Conversos in Guadalupe, Spain* (Princeton, Princeton University Press, 2003), 106. In another case, Rabbi Samuel Valenci was accused of having taught Judaism to a Converso and helped him financially. The Converso in question was known as Rabbi Meir Araye. Yitzhak Baer, *A History of the Jews in Christian Spain: Volume 2* (Philadelphia: Jewish Publication Society, 1961), 342.

[2] Mark D. Meyerson, *A Jewish Renaissance in Fifteenth-Century Spain* (Princeton: Princeton University Press, 2004), 204- 205.

[3] Ibid., 204- 205. Interesting sometime later, this Rabbi Abraham converted. He became known as master Luis and practiced alchemy. Ibid., 215.

hear how many good things and how many prayers and devotions he knew."[4]

The willingness if not eagerness of Jews to help Conversos is evident. Ursula Forcadell requested haroset to celebrate Passover with, and a Jew from Morvedre quickly met her request. Jews also provided matzah to their Conversos family and friends.[5] The significance of eating matzah and drinking kosher wine was not lost on the Church.[6]

When the Converso Joan Domenech was sentenced to death, the Inquisitors noted the following:

"He has made and celebrated the Jewish Passover with Jews, eating matzah for eight days consecutively; and at the head of the table they ate celery and lettuce in the Jewish fashion, and before eating a Jew took bread [matzah] and a cup of wine and he blessed it in the Jewish manner, and then he have a piece of matzah and a sip of wine to the said, Joan Domenech and to the others who were there with him celebrating the said Passover."[7]

Eating at a Jew's home was at times, a semi-communal event for Conversos. In June 1478, Bernat Guimera and his family ate at the home of a Jew and Jewess named Jacob and Perla. The Bernat clan in attendance included Bernat's wife, his daughters and their husbands. Jacob recited brachot which Galceran Ferrantis, Guimera's son in law could not understand. The celebration at Jacob and Perla's home continued with a visit to the synagogue:

"They all went to the synagogue, but they found that it was locked. The said Jew, Jacob, went to look for the Jew who had the key to the synagogue, and he returned with him, and they opened the synagogue. The Jew who had the synagogue key was

---

[4] Ibid., 206.

[5] Ibid., 207.

[6] Regarding the importance of kashrut in preserving Jewish identity, Starr-LeBeau states " Keeping kosher, then, held social as well as spiritual resonances that reinforced its place in family life. This link between kashrut and the home further increased the emotional, social, and spiritual weight behing keeping kosher." Gretchen D. Starr-LeBeau, *In the Shadow of the Virgin: Inquisitors, Friars, and Conversos in Guadalupe, Spain* (Princeton, Princeton University Press, 2003), 68.

[7] Mark D. Meyerson, *A Jewish Renaissance in Fifteenth-Century Spain* (Princeton: Princeton University Press, 2004), 209.

a little, old man…and he showed all the aforesaid [conversos] the synagogue…and they look at a pool which they had covered there with some planks [the mikveh, the ritual bath]. They opened a cabinet where the Torah was kept, and the said old Jew took the Torah in his hands, and it seemed to the witness [Galceran Ferrantis] that he raised it [the Torah] above the heads of all the aforesaid [conversos], of whom some were kneeling, and others were still on their feet. Afterward, the witness saw how the said Cabata opened his purse and took out a piece of gold…and with the said Guimera, his wife, and all others present and watching, he gave the said gold piece to the said Jew who had shown them the Torah, telling him that he was giving him the said gold piece for oil for the lamp of the synagogue."[8]

This type of scenario was apparently not that uncommon. The Conversa Angelina de Leo noted that when she first traveled to Morvedre, "she entered in the said scoles [synagogue] with other people [conversos]…She saw the Torah of the Jews which they showed to her, the said confessant and witness, within a cabinet, just as they used to show them to other people." Mark Meyerson notes that young people were included in these tours. The youths were old enough to understand what they were being introduced to, but still receptive enough to be swayed by the Jewish friends of their parents and elders. Joan Guimera would recall that,

"With my said father and mother and others I entered there [the synagogue] many times and with many youths among whom I recall were the two sons of the late Pere Sanchis- the older was named Joan and the younger Miqualet."

In 1516, the Joan remembered what had transpired 40 years earlier. He stated that "they went to the synagogue of Morvedre, where they knelt and said a prayer, and they ate in the home of a Jew from whom he [Joan] sought penance and forgiveness.[9] In 1489, when questioned by the Inquisition, Violant Guimera argued that her visiting a synagogue was not for religious reasons, but only to see what it was. The Inquisition was not convinced, and she ultimately admitted that she had knelt

---

[8] Ibid., 209.
[9] Ibid., 210.

before the Torah. Moreover, per the testimony of her son, she had been a frequent visitor.

Other Conversos also attempted to legitimize their visits to the synagogue when arrested or questioned by the Inquisition. Pere Alfonso justified his visit to a synagogue on the basis that he only went there to look. He confessed that he had seen the Torah scroll, but argued this was simply in keeping with his free-thinking tendencies. Pere claimed that he had also visited some mosques. Another Converso, Joan Pardo also confessed to visiting a synagogue but stated he had not prayed there since at the time he still believed in the Catholic faith. Aldonca, the widow of Pere Manbrell, admitted that she and Violant looked into the synagogue, but did not perform any ceremonies there. Another Converso, Anthoni Tenca also revealed he and his wife visited a synagogue. While there, he gave alms to a poor Jew but argued he had done nothing else.[10]

The Surrender of Granada by Francisco Pradilla Ortiz

---

[10] Ibid., 211.

The Next Phase

The next stage of the Spanish Inquisition was determined by the last stage of the Reconquista, the conquest of the Muslim Kingdom of Granada which was completed in 1492 by King Ferdinand and Queen Isabella. With the Peninsula now freed from any degree of Muslim hegemony, the monarchs felt free to act on the Jewish question. The lapse of so many Conversos to Judaism was the reason for the expulsion. The purported coaxing of Conversos back to Judaism by Jews and the incomplete work of the Inquisition despite all its efforts prompted the Crown on March 31, 1492, to act decisively. They issued an edict which ordered all Jews to either submit to baptism or leave the kingdom by the last day of July. Jews were permitted to remove property, but no gold, silver, or currency was authorized.[11]

In a desperate attempt to annul the decree, Don Isaac Abravanel offered Ferdinand and Isabella 600,000 crowns for the revocation of the edict. The Grand Inquisitor Torquemada quickly addressed any hesitation that Ferdinand may have had. In what is reported to have been a dramatic scene, Torquemada entered the royal chamber and threw a crucifix down before the king and queen, asking whether like Judas they would give up their Lord for money. Torquemada was determined to sever Conversos from all links to Judaism.[12] Andres Bernaldez relates this view of the Monarchs decision to expel Jews from Spain.

"...y assi con esta junta de estos dos reales ceptros se vengo Nuestro Jesucristo de sus enemigos...los ereges...E por aina dar fin a la eregia musaica le quitaron las raizes que eran las descomulgades sinagogas." ("...And thus Our Lord Jesus Christ took revenge, through the joining of these two royal scepters, on

---

[11] In some cases, as at Vitoria, they took steps to prevent the desecration of the graves of their kindred by presenting the cemetery to the municipality—a precaution not unjustified, as the Jewish cemetery of Seville was later ravaged by the people. The members of the Jewish community of Segovia passed the last three days of their stay in the city in the Jewish cemetery, fasting and wailing over being parted from their beloved dead.

[12] Joseph Perez, *The Spanish Inquisition: A History* (London: Profile Books, 2006), 105.

his enemies...the heretics. And in order to end quickly the Mosaic heresy, they plucked its roots, the banned synagogues."[13]

Expulsión de los Judíos de España by Emilo Sala

The Edict of Expulsion and the Number of the Exiles

The Edict of Expulsion for the Kingdom of Castile states: "You well know that in our dominion, there are certain bad Christians that Judaized and committed apostasy against our Holy Catholic faith, much of it the cause of communications between Jews and Christians. Therefore, in the year 1480, we ordered that the Jews be separated from the cities and towns of our domains and that they be given separate quarters, hoping that by such separation the situation would be remedied. And we ordered that an Inquisition be established in such domains, and in

---

[13] Cited in Eleazar Gutwirth, "The Jews in 15th Century Castilian Chronicles,"The Jewish Quarterly Review, LXXIV. No.4 (1984): 395.

twelve years it has functioned, the Inquisition has found many guilty persons.

Furthermore, we are informed by the Inquisition and others that the great harm done to the Christians persists, and it continues because of the conversations and communications that they have with the Jews, such Jews trying by whatever manner to subvert our holy Catholic faith and trying to draw faithful Christians away from their beliefs.

These Jews instruct these Christians in the ceremonies and observances of their Law, circumcising their children, and giving them books[14] with which to pray, and declaring unto them the days of fasting, and meeting with them to teach them the histories of their Law, notifying them when to expect Passover and how to observe it, giving them the unleavened bread and ceremonially prepared meats, and instructing them in things from which they should abstain, both with regard to food items and other things requiring observances of their Law of Moses, making them understand that there is no other law or truth beside it. All of which then is clear that, on the basis of confessions from such Jews as well as those perverted by them, that it has re-sulted in great damage and detriment of our holy Catholic faith."[15]

It is helpful to quote from the edict of expulsion authored by the In-quisitor General Tomas de Torquemada.

---

[14] Starr-LeBeau writes, "Books in Spanish and Hebrew were another element of individual and collective Judaizing devotions among some New Christians. In addition to playing a key role in Judaism, books provided knowledge normally accessible through one's rabi or learned elders. Some particularly active Judai zers like Martin Gutierrez owned prayer books, possibly in Hebrew, as the above account suggests. Others owned books in Spanish, including Bibles and transla-tions of or variations on Jewish prayers. Two cases of books were seized from Guadalupense conversos and burned at one of the last *autos de fé*, evidence of the importance and availability of books for New Christians trying to observe Judaism." Gretchen D. Starr-LeBeau, *In the Shadow of the Virgin: Inquisitors, Friars, and Conversos in Guadalupe, Spain* (Princeton, Princeton University Press, 2003), 60.

[15] Joseph Perez, *The Spanish Inquisition: A History* (London: Profile Books, 2006), 114.

"It has been proven that they [unconverted Jews] have [through various] means, ways and manners [attempted?] to steal away [Christians] from our Holy Catholic faith and have them depart from it, bringing them and perverting them to their damned beliefs and opinions, instructing them in ceremonies and in observance of their law, making congregations where they read to and taught what they had to do hold and keep and maintain in observance of the said law, arranging for circumcisions for them and for their sons, giving them books in which there were prayers to be made each year, and accompanying them in the temples of their ancestors in order to read and teach them the history of their law, informing them in advance of the festival of Passover, holidays, and mourning days, and advising them of what they had to observe and do, giving them and placing unleavened bread in their hands and meat killed according to their ceremonies in order to celebrate these holidays and festivals, instructing them in things in which they had to partake, such as food and other things, convincing them as much as they could that they had to uphold and keep their law making them understand that the Christian's law was a mockery and the Christian idolaters. All of this was rendered evident and attested to by a great number of witnesses and confessions, by both Jews and those they had perverted and tricked, thus resulting in great damage, detriment to our Holy Catholic faith, according to what has been made public and is known to all in these kingdoms and this bishopric."[16]

---

[16] Ibid. 111-112.

The Alhambra Decree Ordered the Expulsion of Jews from Castile and Aragon

Torquemada's edict was undoubtedly the basis upon which the orders of Castile and Aragon were based. The orders asserted that the continued presence of Jews in Spanish lands presented a major problem for individual Christians. The Christians in question are of course Conversos or their descendants. The claim of the expulsion decree is that Jewish interaction with Conversos caused the latter to lapse into Jewish practices.

According to Henry Kamen, the ultimate goal of the edicts of expulsion was conversion, however. He states:

"From the wording of the decree, it is easy to conclude that this was a total expulsion, giving no alternative and that death and confiscation were the lot of those who came back. Yet there can be absolutely no doubt that the decree had conversion, not expulsion, as it motive, even though not a single word in its offers the alternative."[17]

For the Inquisition, the goal was the elimination of an option for Conversos to revert to Judaism. As long as Jews and synagogues existed in relatively accessible areas, the possibility of interaction remained.[18] In should be noted that in 1480, the Cortes had issued instructions for the complete separation of Jews from their neighbors. From the standpoint of the Inquisition, this was apparently insufficient.

---

[17] Elie Kedourien ed., *Spain and the Jews: The Sephardi Experience 1492 and After* (London: Thames and Hudson, 1992), 81.

[18] Ibid. 80-81.

The actual number of exiles is greatly debated.[19] Andres Bernaldez argued for a total of 160,000 Jews in Castile and Aragon. He stated that 100,000 refugees left Spain and journeyed to Portugal. He also claimed 3,000 from Benevente to Braganza, 30,000 from Zamora to Miranda, 35,000 from Ciudad Rodrigo to Villar, 15,000 from Miranda de Alcantara to Marbao, and 10,000 from Badajoz to Yelves. The contemporary historian Abraham Zacuto estimated 120,000 Jews arrived in Portugal after the edict of expulsion. Approximately 12,000 entered the Kingdom of Navarre, where they were permitted to stay for a brief period.

The ports of Cartagena, Valencia, and Barcelona were designated as ports of exit by King Ferdinand who provided ships to take the departing exiles. Finding welcoming ports was another issue entirely, however. In North Africa in Fez, for example, Jews were denied entry. As a consequence, some even returned to Spain and submitted to baptism when faced with what appeared to be irresolvable circumstances. In another case, nine vessels full of exiles arrived in Naples and spread the plague. In Genoa, Jews were allowed to disembark on the condition they received baptism. Those refugees who eventually reached the Ottoman Empire received a warm welcome from Salim the Sultan.

Financial Challenges, Expulsion, and Conversion

The decree of expulsion left Jews who left financially devastated. Mark Meyerson notes that the attempts of Jews to invest their assets in letters of exchange or to leave money with Christian friends for safe keeping until they could send the money later did not work. The Crown invalidated letters of exchange and seized deposits.[20] Mark Meyerson states:

"Despite King Fernando's rhetorical flourishes concerning the converts having been 'illuminated by the Holy Spirit,' he harbored few illusions as to the sincerity of their Christian beliefs; rather he hoped that, without Jews to influence them, the

---

[19] Singer, Isidore; Adler, Cyrus; (eds.) The Jewish Encyclopedia, "Inquisition: called also Sanctum Officium or Holy Office." Last modified 1904. Accessed January 2, 2013.

[20] Mark D. Meyerson, "Aragonese and Catalan Jewish Converts at the Time of the Expulsion," Jewish History Volume 6. Nos. 1-2 (1992): 132.

neophytes, or at least their children, would become faithful sons and daughters of the Church." [21]

Jewish leaders addressed their remaining financial responsibilities to the Crown and paid off their outstanding debts. This unfortunately created dissension in the community, amidst already difficult circumstances. For example, Jusef Bendeut had been threatened with excommunication if he did not stop disputing his obligation to meet his portion of the Jewish community's debts to the aljama of Ejea de los Caballeros. His son, Miguel de Charitate converted perhaps as a reaction to the aljma's insistence on the financial obligations of his father. [22]

Jews who were already on the fringes of the Jewish community due to criminal or anti-social behavior would likely have been more receptive to the option of baptism since their connections to Judaism were already tenuous. The opportunity to start a life with a new identity may have attracted some. In the case of Juceff Cossen of Monteblanc, after this conversion to Christianity, he was granted his property, and all the legal proceedings against him dropped by the King's directive.

The conversion of people like Rabbi of Borja indeed proved a key factor in the decision of other Jews to opt for baptism. Having seen a community leader convert, many Jews must have questioned the efficacy of continuing in a faith their leaders did not see worthy of keeping. Family ties were a significant factor in the decision of some to convert. A Jewish widower in the town of Tarazona faced the possibility of never seeing his daughter again. She had converted, and this presented him with a difficult choice. In the end, he and his other children converted to Christianity to avoid exile. Juan de Silos argued he had always intended to convert, as he sought to have his property restored to him. Juce Ambron from Huesca left Aragon with his family and mother. After his mother had died, he and his family returned and converted.

For others, family ties were sufficiently strong to convince others to go back to the Peninsula and undergo conversion. Martin Garcia was the eldest son of Astruch Aninay. He was baptized in 1492 and traveled to Genoa the following year to persuade his parents to return to Zaragoza. His parents acquiesced and converted upon their return. Mark Meyerson speculates that some families may have effectively let one of their chil-

---

[21] Ibid., 133.
[22] Ibid., 134-135.

dren convert for the purpose of evaluating the situation after the expulsion. The question of reclaiming property was a critical consideration. In the case of Garcia, he traveled to Genoa only after he had secured rights to his father's property by the hand of the king.[23]

Despite the images of animosity and hatred between Conversos and Jews as depicted by Norman Roth, the fact remained that divided families still maintained family connections with their converted brethren. Myerson argues that the conversion of a family member could prove beneficial to the financial well-being of those that left. Ahim Altortoxi from Huesca demonstrates such a case. Altortoxi sold his possessions to his brother in law who had just converted. There is little uncertainty that Altortoxi fared better financially in doing so that selling to an Old Christian.

Another case is that of Rafael Cavaler of Cervera. He acted as the agent for his brother Simuel who chose to convert. The king granted Rafael permission to take possession of all of Simuel's assets. Meyerson argues this was most certainly done for the purpose of a transfer back to his brother in the form of a bill of exchange.[24]

King Ferdinand and Queen Isabella were relentless in pursuing Converso fugitives fleeing from the Inquisition. In 1488, the monarchs convinced the Kingdom of Navarre to allow the Inquisition to prosecute Conversos in Tudela.[25] In 1498, the Jews of Navarre were landlocked and surrounded by kingdoms which did not permit Jews to enter. With nowhere to go, they converted.

Others escaped only to return. For example, Maria Perez Domech from Huesca initially refused baptism though her husband converted. She fled to Naples. For whatever reason, she returned and was baptized only to find out that her husband had already married another woman. She appealed to the king for her husband to return her dowry.

In Genoa, where no Jewish community existed, some exiles were forced to sell their children as slaves or hire their children out as domestics.[26]

---

[23] Ibid., 135-136.
[24] Ibid., 136.
[25] Ibid., 137.
[26] Ibid., 139.

Once such example is that of the Zaragozan Rabbi Vidal Abnarrabi, who received the name Alfonso Aymerique. After his conversion, he was given a thousand florins from the King, an apparent repayment of a loan extended to the king by Abnarabbi's grandfather. Mark Myerson argues that upper-class Jews had the most to gain by converting to Christianity. Conversely, they also had the most to lose by leaving the peninsula. Interestingly, he argues that poorer Jews were not necessarily motivated to convert since their conversion would only have made them poor Christians.

The chronicler Andres Bernaldez does note that some wealthier Jews assisted poor Jews during the process of leaving the country; nevertheless, some of the poorest Jews converted. Jews in Aragon and Catalonia may have viewed Old Christian society as more receptive than their Castilian counterparts. The Inquisition was most pronounced in Castile, and of course, the earliest purity of blood controversy was raised there. In contrast, the Kingdom of Aragon never saw the kind of violence against Conversos that the Crown of Castile did. So different was the case that Meyerson argues the following:

"...there was an unspoken acceptance of the conversos in the midst- conversos who had achieved the same kind of positions and influence in royal, urban, and ecclesiastical governments for which their Castilian counterparts had earned so much Old Christian hostility- and a relative absence of Castilian-style obsessions with the conversos' political and economic success and their Jewish ancestry."[27]

Aragonese and Catalan Old Christians were apparently aware of Judaizing tendencies or practices among Jewish converts but appear not to have made an issue regarding this before 1483.[28] Meyerson aptly notes the reality of those who converted when he writes:

"One can only speculate about the sincerity of the Jews' conversion to Christianity in 1492 and subsequent years. It would be difficult to argue that these Jews suddenly came to recognition of the truth of Christianity precisely around the time of the expulsion. To say that converts despaired of divine justice and God's

---

[27] Ibid., 142.
[28] Ibid., 142.

concern for the Jewish people is not the same asserting that they received baptism as fully convinced Christians."[29]

Inquisitional activities before 1492 were a warning for Jews who opted to stay that retaining Jewish practice was a dangerous thing.

---

[29] Ibid., 142.

CHAPTER 5

The Kingdom of Portugal

Many Jews from Castile and Aragon fled to the Kingdom of Portugal. Jews in Portugal had escaped the types of violence that Jews in other parts of the Iberian Peninsula had experienced. King Duarte's son, Affonso V reigned from 1438-1481. His reign was well disposed towards Jews of his kingdom. [1]

During his reign, Jews lived outside their designated Jewish quarters. They do not seem to have worn a distinctive badge. They also held public offices. King Affonso V selected Don Isaac Abravanel to be his bursar and minister of finance. Joseph ben David ibn Yahya was held in special favor with the King. The King's disposition towards Jews only increased popular hatred against them. The King also employed Joseph Capateiro of Lamego and Abraham of Beja.

King John II promised to allow Jewish refugees to reside in the Kingdom of Portugal for eight months in return for a tax of 8 crusados to be paid in four installments. He also agreed to provide sufficient ships for them to carry on their voyage to their final destination. In the end, King John II did not keep his commitment.

Anyone who remained in the kingdom after the approved period was enslaved. King John also ordered that little children be taken from their parents who stayed behind. They were sent to the recently discovered

---

[1] Salo Wittmayer Baron, *A Social and the Religious History of the Jews: Volume X* (Philadelphia: Jewish Publication Society, 1965), 213.

island of St. Thomas. Most of most of them died on the ships or died due to the severe conditions of the islands.

After King John's death, his cousin and brother-in-law Dom Manuel was crowned king of Portugal. He ruled from 1495-1521. King Manuel granted freedom to those that had been enslaved during the period of his predecessor. His pending marriage to the daughter of King Ferdinand and Queen Isabella radically changed the situation, however. King Ferdinand and Queen Isabella conceded to the wedding on the condition that King Manuel expel all the Jews from his country. His future bride to be pressed the issue when she stated she would not enter the kingdom of Portugal until the land was purified of Jews.[2]

Their marriage contract was signed on November 30, 1496. On December 4th, King Manuel delivered the edict of expulsion at Muja, near Santarem, ordering that all Jews, regardless of age, leave the kingdom of Portugal by the end of October 1497. Failure to do so was punishable by death and confiscation of property. Any Christian found helping a Jew after the period designated in the decree would forfeit their assets. The edict also mentioned that no future ruler on any pretext whatever was to allow Jews to settle in the kingdom.

King Manual I of Portugal

---

[2] Salo Wittmayer Baron, *A Social and the Religious History of the Jews: Volume X* (Philadelphia: Jewish Publication Society, 1965), 217.

Desperate to keep Jews from leaving the country, the King ordered that all Jewish children, regardless of sex and ranging in age up to twenty years old were to be seized from their parents and brought up as Christians. Bishop D. Fernando Coutinho ardently argued against this compulsory baptism. The forced baptisms were scheduled to being on the first day of the Passover, Sunday, March 19th.

Some parents chose to kill their children to prevent them from undergoing baptism. Bishop Coutinho witnessed a father escort his son to the baptismal font and proclaimed themselves willing martyrs. Isaac ibn Zachin, the son of an Abraham ibn Zachin, killed his children and committed suicide to avert the pending baptism. The King then ordered all remaining Jews to go to Lisbon to board their waiting ships.

Approximately 20,000 persons assembled in the capital. They were corralled into a palace. They were told that the time allocated for their departure had lapsed. As a consequence, they were now the King's slaves. They were visited by the convert Mestre Nicolãom, physician to the queen, and Pedro de Castro, a churchman. Attempts to induce them to convert to Christianity were made but failed. The King then ordered his agents to use force. Many Jews were physically dragged into church by their hair and baptized. Few offered any meaningful resistance. Those few that did were shipped across the sea.

Various Portuguese notables including Bishop Osorius were profoundly stirred by the cruelty of the forced conversions. This disaffection may have prompted Pope Alexander VI to act. The damage was already done. On May 30, 1497, the King adopted a law protecting baptized Jews now known as *christãos novos*, New Christians. They were protected from Inquisitional prosecution for twenty years. The authorities could not accuse them of heresy. When this period expired, any complaint related to Jewish observance would only result in a civil suit being brought against them. If the person in question was convicted, their property passed to their Christian inheritors and not into the fiscal treasury. The possession of Hebrew books was prohibited except for Jewish physicians and surgeons who were permitted to consult Hebrew medical works.[3]

---

[3] The possession of Hebrew books was not the only marker of possible heresy. Even Bibles written in Spanish rather than Latin were considered problematic. Gretchen D. Starr-LeBeau, *In the Shadow of the Virgin: Inquisitors, Friars,*

Some New Christians managed to sell their property and emigrate. The numbers were apparently significant enough to merit regal concern. On April 20th and 21st, 1499, King Manuel prohibited business transactions with New Christians which involved bills of exchange or buying their real estate. They were also forbidden to leave Portugal without royal authorization and captains, and anyone assisting them in fleeing were to be punished. One individual named Goncalo of Loule provided passage to several Conversos from Algarve to Larache in North Africa.[4]

As a consequence of the coerced conversions that followed, New Christians were forced to participate in Church ceremonies. As in Castile, the animosity directed towards Jews was transferred to these New Christians. King Manuel attempted to assuage these new converts to have them sincerely adopt the Christian faith if nothing else out of sheer economic necessity. The ability of the King to shelter them against provocative speeches of zealous priests was limited, nevertheless.

On the 25th of May, 1504 several New Christians met in the Rua Nova, the former Jewish quarter. As they talked, they were encircled by a pack of youths who affronted them. One of the New Christians drew his sword and wounded some of them. Uproar followed but was eventually checked by the appearance of the governor of the city with an armed guard. Forty of the rioters were detained and convicted. They were flogged and were sentenced to be banished to the island of St. Thomas for life. The queen eventually interceded, and they were absolved.

This unrest was followed by the appalling massacre of New Christians in Lisbon in April, 1506. A group of New Christians was attacked, and some were arrested, during the celebration of the Passover on the night of April 17. They were released after two days. The general public was furious at their release and gossiped about bribery having secured their release.

On April 19 another incident occurred when Christians and New Christians attended a service in the Church of the Dominicans. Services were held to pray for the end of a devastating pestilence that had broken

---

and *Conversos in Guadalupe, Spain* (Princeton, Princeton University Press, 2003), 60.

[4] Salo Wittmayer Baron, *A Social and the Religious History of the Jews: Volume XIII* (Philadelphia: Jewish Publication Society, 1969), 46.

out. In a side chapel, a crucifix was reported to radiate an exceptional brilliance. This attracted the attention of Christians, who proclaimed it a miracle. A New Christian voiced his lack of faith in the purported miracle sparking a riot. The New Christian was grabbed by the hair, dragged out of the building, and killed immediately by a mob which included women. His lifeless body was charred on a hurriedly raised pyre on the Rocio Praça. Two Dominican monks, Joaõ Mocho from the city of Evora, and Bernaldo from the Kingdom of Aragonese paraded through the streets carrying a crucifix and shouting "Heresy." They urged the people to eradicate all heretics. The fury of the crowds was added to by German, Dutch, and French sailors in port at the time. The result was an appalling bloodbath.

Lisbon Massacre

On the first day of the violence, over five hundred New Christians were murdered. The following day the cruelties continued. Women and children were not spared. Those attempting to find shelter in the church were pulled from the altar and often burned. Even successful New Christians were not spared. The wealthy tax-farmer Joaõ Rodriguez Mascarenhas was dragged to the Rua Nova and murdered by the mob. At the end of the violence between 2,000 and 4,000 New Christians were killed over the course of forty-eight hours.

The King responded severely by arresting and executing the ringleaders and others involved in the violence. The two Dominican monks involved in the unrest were expelled from their order and strangled.

Their corpses were burned. Any resident found guilty of either theft or homicide was punished corporally and lay open to loss of their property. Friars who had taken part in the uprising were expelled from the monastery. Following the calamity, some New Christians left the kingdom. Some apparently returned to Lisbon and for a time were sheltered by the King.

King Manuel arranged new privileges for New Christians and issued an edict on March 1, 1507, allowing them to leave the country with their property. Those that stayed were reassured by the renewal of the law of May 30, 1497, protecting New Christians from inquisitorial prosecution. On April 21, 1512, it was postponed for an additional period of twenty years. In 1521 the prohibition against emigration under penalty of confiscation of property and loss of freedom was renewed. In 1524, King John accepted a report presented by Jorge Themudo. The report submitted information gathered information from parish priests on the activities of Conversos in their area. The report summarized by the Portuguese historian Alexandre Herculano related that

"...the New Christians ceased to attend divine service on Sundays and religious holidays; that they did not bury their dead in the parish churchyards;...that when close to the death they neither received nor asked for extreme unction.; that in their wills they never provided for masses to be said for their souls;...that they were suspected of observing Saturdays and the ancient Passover;...that they practiced acts of charity among themselves, but not toward the Old Christians;...[yet] they got married at church doors, and baptized their children, observing precisely all the customary rites and solemnities."[5]

Despite this, during the remainder of King Manuel's reign, New Christians did not face further unrest. When King Manual died, his son John III ascended the throne. He ruled from 1521-1557. On December 17, 1531, Pope Clement VII sanctioned the introduction of the Inquisition into the Kingdom of Portugal. Some New Christians now left the country. This occurred particularly under the reign of King Sebastian who ruled from 1557-1578. King Sebastian allowed New Christians to emigrate as long as they paid the enormous sum of 250,000 ducats.

---

[5] Salo Wittmayer Baron, *A Social and the Religious History of the Jews: Volume XIII* (Philadelphia: Jewish Publication Society, 1969), 48.

In 1580, the Spanish Crown seized the Kingdom of Portugal. The new political reality provided some relief to Portuguese New Christians fleeing from the Portuguese Inquisition since they could not be tried in Spanish territory for purported crimes done in the Kingdom of Portugal. The Spanish Inquisition could prosecute, however. Despite this, increased numbers of Portuguese New Christians journeyed to Castile where many of them became successful merchants and some even serving as prominent royal financiers.

Portuguese New Christians now became a central focus of Inquisitional queries. Consequently, the terms distinguishing Portuguese New Christians from Spanish Conversos arose. These terms included portugueses de la nacion hebrea and portugueses de la nacion. These terms were often applied to even Conversos who had been born in Castile but had parents or grandparents with Portuguese origins. The term Portuguese became a synonym for Judaizer.[6]

---

[6] Miriam Bodian, *Hebrews of the Portuguese Nation* (Bloomington: Indiana University Press, 1997), 13.

CHAPTER 6

The Inquisition's Uncompromising Pursuit

E ven bishops were not immune to tribunal investigation. Tomás de Torquemada accused bishops of Jewish descent including Juan Arias Davila, the Bishop of Segovia and Pedro de Aranda, the Bishop of Calahorra of Judaizing.[1] The same was true for friars. In Guadalupe, Fray Alonso de Nogales was accused of being overly sympathetic to Conversos and even encouraging them to Judaize. Fray Pedro de Trujillo testified that Fray Alonso de Nogales had told a recently convert from Judaism named Jeronimo the following:

"[He] should feign with the conversos here who were originally from the place [where he was from] that he was a bad Christian, or that his conversion was fictitious. And thus Jeronimo could take from [the conversos] the most he could. To which I [Fray Pedro de Trujillo] responded, and with some anger, that Jeronimo should not do any such thing, but that he should always show himself to be a true and Catholic Christian with all people and in all places, and that [the other advice] was poor counsel...that later [Jeronimo] should begin, having just been baptized, to do that

---

[1] Again the exact numbers become a matter of disagreement, but during his term as chief inquisitor perhaps more than 8,000 Conversos were burned at the stake. Another 6,000 were burned in effigy.

which all these evil heretics had had and done, that is, with Jews show themselves to be Jews, and with Christian Christians."[2]

Diego Deza succeeded Torquemada as Grand Inquisitor. On February 22, 1501, an *auto da fé* was held in Toledo which saw 38 persons burned. All of the victims were from Herrera. The next day 67 women from Herrera and Alcocen were burned in Toledo. Concomitant with this was the execution at the stake of another 90 Conversos in Cordoba. On March 30, 1501, a further 9 people were burned in Toledo. Another 56 men and 87 women were sentenced to life imprisonment. In July, Seville also saw 45 persons burned in Seville. Despite his zeal, Diego Deza, of Jewish descent on his mother's side, was even accused of Judaizing. Because of Diego Deza's illness, Bishop Juan of Vigue was appointed grand inquisitor of Aragon and Francisco de Ximenes, the Archbishop of Toledo was named Grand Inquisitor of Castile.

Diego de Deza by Francisco de Zurbarán

---

[2] In Guadalupe, 21 out of 130 friars were found guilty of Judaizing. Gretchen D. Starr-LeBeau, *In the Shadow of the Virgin: Inquisitors, Friars, and Conversos in Guadalupe, Spain* (Princeton, Princeton University Press, 2003), 103-105, 217.

Diego Deza's most ruthless inquisitor, in turn, was Diego Rodriguez Lucero, the inquisitor of Córdoba. Lucero's tactics and cruelty were so renowned that Gonzalo de Avora wrote to the royal secretary Almazan on July 16, 1507. De Avora wrote:

"Deza, Lucero, and Juan de la Fuente have dishonored all provinces; they have no regard either for God or for justice; they kill, steal, and dishonor girls and women to the disgrace of the Christian religion."[3]

Lucero meticulously accused any individual he suspected of Jewish ancestry. This included the Archdeacon de Castro, whose father was a Converso. Between December 1504 and May 1506, up to one hundred and twenty persons were burned. Another one hundred followed in June 1506. Lucero's tactics gained notoriety, and his fervor was characterized as primarily focused on the confiscation of property as the Bishop of Córdoba and many notables related in a complaint sent to the Pope. Lucero even prosecuted the sister and nephews of Hernando de Talavera, the Archbishop of Granada.[4] The contempt for Deza Lucero was demonstrated by a request from leading citizens of Córdoba to the inquisitor-general Deza seeking his removal.

A petition was issued to Queen Juana and Philip of Austria, her husband. On September 30, 1505, Philip and Juana addressed Deza and harshly criticized Lucero's measures. The Inquisition was suspended until their return to Spain. Philip died abruptly, and Lucero was confident enough to assert that the majority of the knights and nobles of Córdoba and other cities were, in fact, Judaizers and maintained synagogues in their homes. Lucero went too far, and the Marquis of Priego rallied forces and attacked an Inquisitional prison. Priego released prisoners and arrested the procurator, though Lucero managed to escape. Lucero was ultimate arrested and his actions investigated.[5]

In Rome, Conversos bribed the Curia and even offered 100,000 ducats to King Ferdinand if he suspended the Inquisition until the arrival of

---

[3] Singer, Isidore; Adler, Cyrus; (eds.) The Jewish Encyclopedia, "Inquisition: called also Sanctum Officium or Holy Office." Last modified 1904. Accessed January 2, 2013. goo.gl/SX6f8D

[4] Joseph Perez, *The Spanish Inquisition: A History* (London: Profile Books, 2006), 59.

[5] Ibid., 59.

the new royal couple. Despite the fact that an investigation was launched into his conduct, Lucero nevertheless accused Hernando de Talavera, the Archbishop of Granada, who had Jewish ancestry, and his whole family, of Judaizing. De Talavera's relatives had been imprisoned.[6] De Talavera, the former confessor of Queen Isabella, was forced to go barefoot and bareheaded in a procession through the streets of Granada. The elements were too much to bear for De Talavera, and he caught a fever and succumbed five days later.

After Philip's death, King Ferdinand re-ascended the throne of Castile and finally dismissed Deza. This was primarily to curtail the opposition against the Inquisition that had gathered in Córdoba and Ximenes. Archbishop of Toledo was appointed inquisitor-general in June 1507. Ximenes directed an investigation and in May 1508, determined to incarcerate Lucero. The commission assembled to investigate the charges against Lucero gave orders that all those imprisoned on the charge of Judaizing by Lucero were to be released.[7]

Charles V and Inquisitional Policy

The grand inquisitor Cardinal Ximenes de Cisneros continued a vigilant policy against Judaizing though with less controversy. A few years after his death, prominent Conversos sent a deputation to King Charles in Flanders requesting that the powers of the Inquisition be restricted, and testimony be presented in public. With opposition to Charles I active in Castile, Conversos hoped that a substantial financial inducement would convince him. In 1509 the Inquisitorial tribunal of Valladolid instructed the University not to grant degrees to individuals who had

---

[6] According to a chronicler, when Talavera tried to convert Jews to Christianity he found "'[Jews] are naturally clear and can quote the Holy Scripture so readily, they often argued against what preached to them was whereas most people apparently simply accepted it." Toby Green, *Inquisition: The Reign of Fear* (New York: St. Martin's Press, 2007), 270.

[7] Henry C. Lea, "Lucero, the Inquisitor," American Historical Review ii (1897): 611-626; See also Jose Amador de Los Rios, *Historia Socia, Politica y Religiosa de los Judios de Espana y Portugal, Volume 3* (Madrid: T. Fortanet, 1876), 483.

recently converted from Judaism in accordance with the purity of blood statutes.[8]

Procession of Herectics by Francisco Goya Lucientes

Spanish resentment against Conversos was a mere reflection of enduring anti-Jewish sentiments. They continued to exist even after Jews were baptized. The real and perceived ambiguities about Converso identity disrupted the purported boundaries between Christians and Jews.[9] Charles V was however against any papal modifications to the structure of the Inquisition. On September 24, 1519, he wrote to Lope Hurtado de Mendoza, his ambassador in Rome the following:

"...the nefarious and abominable things which have been committed against our holy Catholic faith. Since our arrival in these Our kingdoms of the Crown of Aragon [April 24, 1518], two synagogues, concealed for a long time, have been discovered, where some persons of *that race* [generacion] assembled in order

---

[8] Kevin Ingram, "Secret lives, public lies: the conversos and socio-religious non-conformism in the Spanish Golden Age." (PhD diss., UC San Diego, 2006), 132. Conviction for heresy also had longer term consequences. Even if an individuals was reconciled to the Church they remained ineligible for certain public and clerical posts. One way to address this problem was to "buy back" their honor by paying the Crown a composition fine. From 1494 to 1497 alone, more than five thousand cases of Conversos paying to have their honor restored are documented. Joseph Perez, *The Spanish Inquisition: A History* (London: Profile Books, 2006), 129.

[9] Miriam Bodian, *Hebrews of the Portuguese Nation* (Bloomington: Indiana University Press, 1997), 7.

to Judaize under the direction of a rabbi who instructed them in the law of Moses."[10]

The Papacy' relationships with Conversos was a complicated affair. During the reign of Pope Alexander VI (July 23, 1498), 280 Conversos had admitted their Judaizing practices in Rome publicly. However, Conversos were even more firmly positioned in Pope Leo's court. There several Conversos who had fled the Inquisition, Diego de Las Casas, Juan Gutierrez, and Bernaldino Diez served as courtiers.[11]

Purity of lineage became a key obsession of Spanish society, and hence greater focus was placed on the Conversos' shared ethnic origins. Old Christians believed that the predilection to Judaize was reflective of natural racial features. Despite the intensity of the Inquisition in its first years of operation, as time passed, fears of Judaizing only increased. As long as the tainted blood of Conversos continued to exist, the subversion of Christian society was always a possibility. The adoption of purity of blood statutes strengthened these perceptions. They created a separate and inferior social status for those with Jewish backgrounds. Conversos regardless of whether they adopted Christianity sincerely or not, they now faced potential exclusion from military orders, religious orders, municipal councils, and guilds. The statutes were not always strictly enforced but nevertheless presented a real issue for Conversos.[12]

Several converts including Luis Gutierrez along with Diego de las Casas and Bernaldino Diez worked to secure the favor of the Curia. Pope Leo X extended a bull per their request. As soon as Charles heard of the bull, he attempted to stop its publication. Charles sent word to Leo X via Lope Hurtado de Mendoza, his envoy that the complaints of the Conversos were bases. The new Inquisitor-General for Castile, Adrian, and the former Bishop of Tortosa, appointed on May 4, 1518, was disposed towards restraint and proper procedure.

Charles further revealed that Conversos who complained about the Inquisition had offered him a large sum of money to restrain the tribunal. This was the same tactic they had tried with his grandfather, Ferdi-

---

[10] Salo Wittmayer Baron, *A Social and the Religious History of the Jews: Volume XIII* (Philadelphia: Jewish Publication Society, 1969), 92.

[11] Ibid., 92.

[12] Miriam Bodian, *Hebrews of the Portuguese Nation* (Bloomington: Indiana University Press, 1997), 11.

nand. Charles avowed that under no conditions would the bull be distributed in his kingdom. The Pope acceded to Charles's demand, and the Inquisition continued its operations unimpeded.

There were tribunals in Seville, Córdoba, Jaen, Toledo, Valladolid, Calahorra, Llerena, Saragossa, Valencia, Barcelona, Cuenca, Granada, and Tudela until Until 1538. At Palma in the Balearic Isles, the first *auto da fé* was held in 1506. 22 Judaizers were burned in effigy. Several Jews were burned alive in 1509 and 1510, and 62 Judaizers were burned in effigy in the following year.[13]

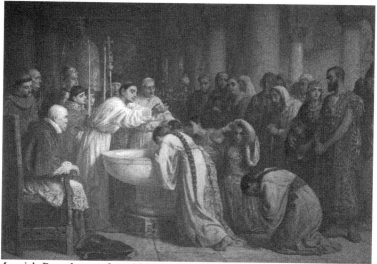

The Moorish Proselytes of Archbishop Ximenes, Granada in 1500 by Edwin Long

The Inquisition under the Reign of the Philips

From 1478 until 1524, the Spanish Inquisition was focused on Judaizing. From The Inquisition processed thousands of Judaizing cases and continued to do so for centuries. The Inquisition turned its attention to the rise of Protestantism, the Alumbrados, Muslim converts to Christianity, and other groups.[14]

---

[13] Singer, Isidore; Adler, Cyrus; (eds.) The Jewish Encyclopedia, "Inquisition: called also Sanctum Officium or Holy Office." Last modified 1904. Accessed January 2, 2013.

[14] Joseph Perez, *The Spanish Inquisition: A History* (London: Profile Books, 2006), 61.

The Inquisition continued its operation unimpeded under the reign of the Philip dynasty, albeit in a slightly less conventional fashion. Under the reign of Philip II, Fernando de Valdes, the former Archbishop of Seville was known for the ruthlessness of his operations. His actions and tactics were protested heavily by the Cortes. Their demands for the tribunals to be restricted were unheeded. The same was the case under the reign of Philip III. Attempts to restrain its activities by Duke de Olivares under Philip III also proved fruitless. Under the reign of Philip III as well as under Philip IV Conversos continued to be condemned to the stake throughout the kingdom. Each tribunal convened at least one *auto da fé* each year.

The Burning of Protestants in Valladolid May 21[st,] 1559

The primary number occurred in the cities of Seville, Granada, and Córdoba. Grand *autos da fe* were held in Córdoba on December 3, 1625, May 3, 1655, and June 29, 1665. Among those burned at the first of these was Manuel Lopez, who adamantly resisted all attempts at conversion. The last *auto* lasted saw 55 Judaizers burned. 3 of the former were burned alive. 16 were burned in effigy. In 1631, between May 6 and May 28, five *autos da fé* had been held at Palma including the burning of 25 Conversos from Palma on the first of the *autos*. 210 Conversos were also condemned to life imprisonment. Under the reign of Philip IV, a tribunal was instituted in the new capital of Madrid on July 4, 1632.

Under the forty-six year reign of Philip V, the Inquisition's tribunal held one and at times two or three *autos* a year for those accused of Judaizing. On November 30, 1719, fourteen people charged with Judaizing appeared at the *auto da fé* held in Badajoz.[15] In 1720 it renewed its efforts. In 1722 three *autos da fé* were held in Seville while two in Murcia and Cuenca. In 1723, three took place in Granada, and two occurred in the cities of Valladolid, Toledo, and Cuenca. During the reign of Philip V, a further 1,564 persons were burned, with a further 782 burned in effigy.

11,730 persons were also sentenced to a variety of punishments which ranged from short-term imprisonments of six months to life imprisonment. Ninety percent of these were accused of Judaizing. By the reigns of Ferdinand VI and Charles III, Inquisitional activity was more restricted. Judaizers were no longer burned at the stake. *Autos da fé* became fewer.

As Joseph Perez notes, by 1750, the primary impetus for Inquisition had ceased to exist. Its prosecution of tens of thousands of Judaizers, Protestants, and various non-conformists sects had largely accomplished its goals. Perez states, "There simply were no longer any Protestants, non-conformists, or Illuminist sects in Spain." The Inquisition continued to prosecute witches, bigamists, and other heretics, but the Institution now operated primarily as a political entity which focused on combating liberal ideas.[16]

King Joseph Bonaparte ended the Inquisition's reign in 1808, but to universal surprise Ferdinand VII reinstituted it. Only in 1834 did the tribunals of the Inquisition disappear entirely from Spain.

The New World

Spain's discovery and conquest of the New World provided a venue for Conversos to find refuge and avoid the Inquisitional authority, though this proved short lived. Though the Inquisition was not formally established in Mexico until 1571, the first victim of Judaizing in the New World was Hernan Alonso, burned in 1528. Alonso was among Hernan Cortes' conquistadors who participated in the conquest of Mexico. In the case of Francisco Pizarro's conquest of the Incan empire, at least three Conversos, Machine de Florencia, Pedro del Paramo, and

---

[15] Ibid., 40.

[16] Joseph Perez, *The Spanish Inquisition: A History* (London: Profile Books, 2006), 93-94.

Pedro de San Millan, have been identified among his small army. So significant was the presence of Conversos in the New World, which the Inquisitor would report back to his superiors:

"I attest to your Excellencies [certifico a U.S.] that Lima and the entire realm has been full of a great many conversos and sons and grandsons of reconciled persons. In relation to the few Spaniards who live in these parts, there are twice as many conversos as in Spain."[17]

In 1574, the first *auto da fé* was held, and between 1574 and 1593 nine autos were held. The *auto da fé* held on December 8, 1596, included 60 penitents and victims including members of the famed Carvajal family. [18] The *auto de fé* of March 25, 1602, included more than 100. In 1608 Jorge de Almeida was excommunicated and in 1645 Gabriel de Granada was sentenced. In 1646, 71 persons, primarily accused of Judaizing, appeared at the *auto da fe*. Two additional *autos da fes* were held in 1648 and 1649. In 1659 Diego Diaz and Francisco Botello were also burned for Judaizing. [19]

Inquisitional tribunals were also established in Lima and Cartagena. One of the first victims in Lima in around the year 1581 was the physician Juan Alvarez of Zafra. He along with his wife, children, and father, were executed for Judaizing. The same was the case for Manuel Lopez, also known as Luis Coronado. An *auto da fé* was held in Lima on January 23, 1639. 63 Judaizers appeared, and 11 were burned. Included among these were Francisco Maldonado de Silva, and Diego Lopez de Fonseca. In total, 129 *autos da fés* were held in the New World with several thousand cases tried for various crimes. Both tribunals were abolished in 1820.

---

[17] Salo Wittmayer Baron, *A Social and the Religious History of the Jews: Volume XIII* (Philadelphia: Jewish Publication Society, 1969), 139.

[18] Seymour Leibman, *The Jews in New Spain: Faith, Flame, and the Inquisition*, (Coral Gables: University of Miami Press, 1970), 178-179.

[19] George Alexander Kohut, *Jewish Martyrs of the Inquisition in South America* (New York: The Friedenwald Company, 1895), 21.

CHAPTER 7

The Inquisition in Portugal

K ing John III who ruled Portugal from 1521-1557, pushed for the establishment of the Inquisition. He was supported in this endeavor by Queen Catherine, the granddaughter of Isabella and in particular by a Converso named Henrique Nunes. Nunes argued that the majority of the Conversos remained loyal to Judaism at heart. Nunes strongly urged the institution of the tribunal.

Conversos had already been subjected to execution for Judaizing in Portugal even before the introduction of the Inquisition. Five Conversos found guilty of observing the Law of Moses were burned in Olivença, under the purview the Bishop of Ceuta, a former Franciscan. The event was coupled with a bull-fight to celebrate the event.

The introduction of the Inquisition in Portugal was also pressed forward by the appearance of David Reubeni. He was joined by a Portuguese Converso named Diogo Pires who changed his name to Solomon Molko.1 Solomon Molko adopted a messianic message of redemption which was powerful enough to undertake a rescue of several women under the custody of the Spanish Inquisition. The daring nature of this action infuriated the inquisitor Selayo of Badajoz. He wrote to the King on March 30, 1528, pleading him to follow the example of Spain and to eliminate the Judaizing heresy among Conversos. Concurrent with the daring rescue, other Conversos in Gouvea were accused of having de-

---

[1] Salo Wittmayer Baron, *Social and Religious History of the Jews, Volume XIII* (New York: Columbia University Press, 1958), 49.

filed an image of the Virgin and momentum to move to take action against them.

The King was finally persuaded by these events and by the appeals from his queen and powerful lords. He acquiesced to the introduction of the Inquisition on Portuguese territory. The King commissioned Bras Neto the ambassador at the Curia, to petition Pope Clement VII for a bull authorizing the tribunal's establishment.

The request was surprisingly opposed by Cardinal Lorenço Pucci who argued candidly that King John was just emulating Ferdinand and Isabella's real motivation behind the creation of the Inquisition. This motivation according to Pucci was to appropriate Conversos' wealth and property. Cardinal Lorenço Pucci's opposition was fleeting due to his death shortly afterward. The bull was obtained on December 17, 1531. The Franciscan Diogo da Silva, the confessor of King John III, was appointed Grand Inquisitor.

Diogo da Silva

While permission was extended to Portugal to establish its tribunal, its operation was delayed. Diogo da Silva refused to accept his appointment. Many Conversos were kept informed of the proceedings in Rome.

Some made preparations to flee. Conversos were hindered, however, by a law issued by King John on June 14, 1532, which made it illegal for them to leave the country. Anyone aiding Conversos attempting to escape would face confiscation of their property. Any captain who transported Conversos was sentenced to death.

The Bull of Pardon of 1533

Individual Conversos organized and sent Converso Duarte de Paz to Rome as their emissary. De Paz was remarkably successful in his endeavors and was able to obtain a suspension of the bull. His efforts continued when on October 17, 1532, it was abrogated. On April 7, 1533, a bull of pardon was issued.

The Pope declared, contrary to previous Church teaching, that Jews who had been baptized by force were not members of the Church. Their continued observance of Jewish practices was therefore not heretical. Those individuals who had those who had been willingly brought to the Church by their parents were Christians, however. They were to be treated with kindness and won over to Christianity through gentleness and love. The papal edict stated that all Conversos covered by the edict of pardon were also allowed to leave the country with their possessions.

However, King John was determined to prevent the publication of the bull and disregarded the threats of excommunication for failing to implement it. He sent Dom Henriquez de Menezes as his ambassador to Rome to appeal its implementation. Cardinal Santiquatro assisted Menezes and ordered the establishment of a commission, consisting of the Cardinals Campeggio and De Cesis to investigate the matter. Consequently, Clement issued a new declaration on April 2, 1534. A few months later on July 26, another statement was made to the Nuncio in Lisbon.[2] It ordered him to publish the bull of April 7, 1533, without any postponement. All Conversos then imprisoned were to be released.

Continued Struggles under the Inquisition

King John continued his attempts to have the papal edict repealed. The Spanish ambassador in Rome, Count de Cifuentas, and Cardinal

---

[2] The Nuncio was responsible for disseminating papal announcements.

Santiquatro acted on his appeal. However, while Duarte de Paz and Diogo Rodriguez-Pinto represented Conversos in Rome, the new Pope Paul III decided in November 1534; the Bulle de Perdon was not published for the time being.

Paul III submitted the controversy to a new commission for additional investigation. This committee included Cardinal Hieronymo Ghenucci, the author of a work in defense of the Conversos. The majority of the new board surprisingly articulated a position favorable to the Conversos. Concurrently, the Bulle de Perdon was published throughout Portugal. The Papal Nuncio, however, related that the King refused to release Conversos in custody and had, in fact, made additional arrests. On June 14, 1535, the King renewed the law barring Converso mass departure for three years. The Pope responded by issuing a statement on July 20, 1535. The report related that anyone hindering the flight of the Conversos was subject to excommunication.

Pope Paul III tried to broker a compromise with King John was tried by on the advice of Diogo Rodriguez-Pinto. The deal entailed a pardon to all Conversos, including those currently in custody. Conversos were be permitted to leave the country in a year. Were King John to agree to these terms, the Pope would, in turn, sanction the King's introduction of the Inquisition unimpeded. Despite the seemingly favorable terms, King John declined to make any concessions.

Pope Paul III's Bull of October 12, 1535

King John's unwillingness to comply was met by the similar tenaciousness of Pope Paul III. On October 12, 1535, Pope Paul III released a new and weightier bull, similar to the Bulle de Perdon which had been issued on April 7, 1533. The bull dismissed all suits brought against Conversos. It also canceled every confiscation of property initiated against them. All sentences against them without regard to the place of residence or any statements made by them were also annulled. This bull was published throughout the country.

King John and the Infante Affonso finally acquiesced and released the Conversos then in detention.[3] The Pope endorsed the establishment of the tribunal with certain conditions. The Inquisition was not to operate as an independent institution. Evidence provided by servants and convicts was prohibited. Perhaps most significantly was the caveat that the testimony of witnesses was not to be kept secret and that the property of heretics was not to be transferred to the state's coffers. Accusations were also not to be levied against the deceased.[4]

Despite King John's previous acquiescence, he refused to agree to these conditions. He turned to Emperor Charles V, his brother-in-law, to appeal the pope. Charles V visited Rome in April 1536 celebrating a recent victory over the Ottoman Turks. He asked the Pope to grant King John's demand for the creation of an Inquisition without stipulations. Pope Paul refused. He continued to argue that the Conversos of Portugal could not be regarded as Christians.

The Papal Bull of May 23, 1536

The attempts of the Conversos to thwart King John's machinations through the efforts of Duarte de Paz stalled due to their inability to raise a sufficient bribe for the Roman Curia. Without success, the nuncio Della Ruvere attempted to confer with wealthy Conversos in Evora. Ruvere also contacted the well-to-do Diogo Mendes, who had previously provided funds on behalf of Conversos in need.

Pope Paul's courageous defiance of the Emperor began to falter, however. The Pope was pressed by the Portuguese ambassador at Rome, Alvare Mendes de Vasconcellos. Mendes pushed for a decision and a resolution to the impasse. On May 23, 1536, the Pope gave in and issued a bull in which the establishment of the Inquisition in Portugal was

---

[3] Singer, Isidore; Adler, Cyrus; (eds.) The Jewish Encyclopedia, "Inquisition: called also Sanctum Officium or Holy Office." Last modified 1904. Accessed January 2, 2013.

[4] Ibid.

announced. The bulls of April 7, 1533, and October 12, 1535, were repealed.[5]

Despite having agreed to allow the Inquisition to operate, Pope Paul III managed to ensure that for its first three years of operations, it would follow the procedure of civil courts. The names of accusers and witnesses were to be concealed from the accused. During the first ten years of the tribunal's operation, the property of those condemned would be transferred to their nearest relatives. John seemingly agreed to these conditions.

Before the Inquisition began its operation, the inquisitor general Diogo da Silva issued a decree which required all Conversos to make a complete confession of faith in thirty days. They were promised a full pardon if they complied. Two of the most influential Conversos of Lisbon, Jorge Leaõ, and Nuño Henriquez attempted to persuade the Infante Louis, the King's brother to extend the amnesty period to one year. Louis and the King refused to grant the extension. The Conversos continued their appeals to the Pope to repeal his previous bull of May 23. The Conversos stated:

"If your Holiness should disregard the petitions and the tears of the Jewish nation, which we do not indeed expect, we hereby swear before God and before your Holiness with loud lamentations, and we solemnly declare before the whole world, that, since no place has been found where we have been admitted among Christians and since we, our honor, our children, our flesh, and blood, have been persecuted; though we have tried to abstain from Judaism, if hereafter tyranny does not cease, we will do that which not one of us would otherwise have thought of; namely, we will return to our Mosaic religion and will abandon Christianity, through the teachings of which we have been forced to take this step. We solemnly declare this, in the face of the cruelty to which we are sacrificed; we will make use of the right assured to us by your Holiness, by the cardinal protector, and by the ambassadors of Portugal, and we will all

---

[5] Singer, Isidore; Adler, Cyrus; (eds.) The Jewish Encyclopedia, "Inquisition: called also Sanctum Officium or Holy Office." Last modified 1904. Accessed January 2, 2013.

leave our old homes to seek safety and protection among less cruel peoples."[6]

Attempts to Prevent the Inquisition's Operation

Despite setbacks their attempt to curtail the Inquisition's ability to operate, they did receive considerable support by the nuncio Della Ruvere. Ruver approached the Pope and successfully represented King John's plans. He persuaded the Pope to grant a bull, and it was issued on May 23, 1536, to a commission of inquiry and review. This review board comprised of Cardinal Ghinucci, Jacobacio, and Cardinal Simoneta. Hieronymo Ricenati Capodiferro, a new nuncio, was sent to Portugal to shield the Conversos and ensure that the King satisfied the agreement.

The Pope appeared to regain his potency as complaints from Conversos were received and related the brutal treatment which they had experienced. The Pope in February 1537 called upon King John, to lift his band on emigration of Conversos under pain of excommunication. Through Capodiferro's actions, Conversos were released from the Inquisition's jails. Some of those released from prison escaped to the Ottoman Empire and North Africa. The Inquisition was checked for the moment.

The Lisbon Placard

The relative peace was short lived. In February 1539, notices were placed on the doors of various cathedrals and churches in Lisbon. They stated: "The Messiah has not come. Jesus was not the true Messiah." The King and Capodiferro were prompted to action. They offered rewards of several thousand cruzados for determining the author of this decree. Many Conversos were concerned. In a rather weak attempt to throw off suspicion, they posted a subsequent proclamation on a cathedral door stating: "I, the author, am neither a Spaniard nor a Portuguese,

---

[6] Ibid.

but an Englishman; and if instead of 10,000 you should offer 20,000 escudos, you would not discover my name."[7]

In the end, a Converso named of Manuel da Costa was arrested. Tortured, he confessed. His hands were cut off, and then he was publicly burned in Lisbon. The respite that Conversos had enjoyed ended. Diogo da Silva was removed due to his leniency. In his stead, the Cardinal Infante Henrique, a brother of the King, was selected as Grand Inquisitor. John of Mello and the John Soares were also appointed as Inquisitors. To ensure that his policies would be accepted in Rome, King John sent Pedro Mascarenhas as ambassador to Rome with the purpose of convincing the Curia. The Pope, however, remained resolute in opposing King John's plans.

The Papal Bull of October 12, 1539

The Pope insisted on recalling the newly appointed inquisitor-general, Cardinal Infante Henrique. The Pope received reports regarding the tribunal's brutality. He issued a new bull on October 12, 1539. The Pope insisted that the names of accusers and witnesses be disclosed to the accused. False witnesses were to be punished. Most significantly, no one was to be indicted by confessions made under torture. Any commutation of a sentence versus a loss of goods was prohibited without the agreement of the condemned. Appeals to Rome were permitted at all times.

However, the Papal bull was left unpublished, and King John operated the Inquisition as he wished. In a communiqué to Mascarenhas, his ambassador, he proposed renouncing all claims to property of the condemned for ten years. In return, he requested that the Pope grant the Portuguese Inquisition the same independence which characterized the Spanish Inquisition.

---

[7] Singer, Isidore; Adler, Cyrus; (eds.) The Jewish Encyclopedia, "Inquisition: called also Sanctum Officium or Holy Office." Last modified 1904. Accessed January 2, 2013.

The First Portuguese Auto da Fé

Dom Henrique remained Grand Inquisitor, and the Holy Office continued its activity when the papal edict of October 12, 1539, was not published, The first tribunals were established in the cities of Lisbon, Evora, and Coimbra. The first *auto da fé* in Lisbon was held on October 23, 1541. This court's authority extended over Alemtejo and Algave. The Evora tribunal condemned David Reubeni and Luis Dias to death. The latter claimed to be the Messiah.

An Auto da fé in Lisbon's Terreiro do Paco

Conversos tried mitigating the growing power of the Inquisition. They tried arranging another nuncio sent to Portugal. They raised large sums and placed them at the disposal of their agent in Rome, Diogo Fernandez Neto. He successfully gained the support of Cardinal Parisio. Parisio while in Bologna during the second and third sessions of the Consil pro Christianis Noviter Conversis had argued the following:

"By reason and law, that considering they [the Jews] were forced to accept baptism and were not converted willingly, they had not fallen, nor do they fall, under any censure."[8]

Neto approached the Pope and offered to donate 10,000 cruzados and to support the nuncio with 250 crusados every month were a new nuncio appointed. The Pope was urged to accept the offer by Cardinals Parisio and Carpi. Nevertheless, it appears that only after a fiery dispute be-

---

[8] Ibid.

tween the Pope and De Sousa that the former determined to assign a new nuncio.

Luis Lippomano, the Bishop of Bergamo was chosen for the position. King John soon took advantage of an unanticipated event. Luis Lippomano had not reached Lisbon when letters were found which gravely compromised the agents of the Conversos, the new nuncio, and even the Pope.

The situation was a disaster. The nuncio was now incapable of doing anything for the Conversos. Neto was arrested and sat in prison. The majority of the cardinals, as well as the future Pope Paul IV, supported the King. Conversos responded by sending new agents to Rome.

The Papal Bull of August 22, 1546

Under his administration, permanent tribunals were ultimately established in Lisbon, Evora, Coimbra, Porto, Lamego, and Tamar. By 1560, an overseas branch had also been set up in Goa.[9] The Inquisitional activity which began in Coimbra spread throughout the province of Beira rapidly. Agents were sent to Trancoso where many wealthy Conversos lived. Many Conversos escaped to the mountains. Approximately thirty-five persons, many of them elderly and infirmed, who had been incapable of fleeing, were arrested.

In Evora, Pedro Alvares de Paredes was appointed Inquisitor. He was particularly successful in extracting confessions from the accused. In particular cases, he even forged letters and read forged decisions to the prisoners. Prisoners faced with this purported evidence readily admitted whatever he demanded of them to avoid further punishment.

In Lamego, the Inquisition began operations in late 1542. Many Conversos fled to Tras-os-Montes. Their efforts proved fruitless, as they were brought back to Lamego. A Tribunal was also established in the city of Porto. In Porto, Balthasar Limpo, the Carmelite Bishop of the diocese, was selected as Inquisitor. Limpo was committed to a war of total annihilation against the Conversos as a recognizable class. Limpo was resolute in his mission and even hired criminals and prostitutes to testify against Conversos. Large numbers of Conversos were jailed to

---

[9] Salo Wittmayer Baron, *A Social and the Religious History of the Jews: Volume XIII* (Philadelphia: Jewish Publication Society, 1969), 53.

the extent that in Lisbon the Estaõs, located on the Rocio place, and numerous municipal buildings were used as prisons.

Efforts by Conversos to influence the Pope at last proved successful. Pope Paul III once again opposed the extent of the violence and excesses by the Portuguese Inquisition. The Pope appointed a new nuncio. Cardinal Ricci de Monte Policiano was installed as nuncio. King John, however, stalled the arrival of the new nuncio. His entry into Lisbon occurred only after an extended exchange between the royal court and the Curia during September 1545.

Cardinal Ricci moved quickly and harshly rebuked the Cardinal-Infante, the King, and the prelates for the brutal practices of the Inquisitors. Ricci's actions reignited the fight between King John and the Curia. This was augmented by the Pope's new bull on August 22, 1546. This extended the duration of the terms stipulated in the bull of May 23, 1536, for twelve month periods. The confiscation of Converso property was prohibited for ten more years.

The King submitted to the Pope's directive. In a surprise move, he requested that four of the most famous Conversos form a commission to delineate the circumstances under which genuine Conversos would submit to a religious tribunal. In January 1547, the Conversos requested the King implement the pardon which had been previously put into effect. They also asked that the procedures of the Inquisition be restrained. They also implored that the identities of accusers and witnesses should be revealed to those accused.[10]

---

[10] Memorial of the Conversos, January, 1547: "If we should be granted peace, all Conversos who are now in the country would stay here and those also who are wandering in Galicia and Castile, and many of those who have already settled in Flanders, Italy, and other lands would return; they would establish business houses and resuscitate the commerce, which is now prostrate... The severity of the Spanish Inquisition ought not to be taken as a model. The Portuguese resolve to leave home more quickly; it would be in vain to forbid them to emigrate. Experience has shown how readily they abandon property and everything else and with what fearlessness they defy every danger in order to escape from their birthplace. Without moderation and tolerance few of us will remain in the country. Even in Castile we are not ill-treated until we have been found guilty of some crime. . . . To this extent our fellow believers exposed themselves to the dangers of the inquisition and nevertheless how many escaped from Spain? At present those who flee from Portugal are hospitably received in the

The Submission of the Curia

The requests crafted by the Conversos were submitted to the inquisitors for review and approval. Despite the prompting of the King, the Inquisition would not entertain any possibility or idea of concessions or leniency. At an impasse, the Curia moved to declare a general pardon for all Conversos who publicly confessed their observance of Jewish practices. Concurrently, the Curia tried to convince the King to grant Conversos a year to leave the kingdom without obstruction. The King, however, refused to agree to any of these proposals.

The Pope was unable to press the matter any further. Faced with the resoluteness of the King, he acquiesced. He designated Ugoino, a nephew of Cardinal Santiquatro, as commissioner to convey three bulls which related the Pope's approbation of the Inquisition and the terms of the pardon. No other leniencies or indulgences would be granted to Conversos. The Converso attempts to stymied Inquisitional power in Portugal proved ineffective, though they managed to delay its full operation by twenty years.

On July 10, 1548, the pardon mutually agreed to by the Pope and King was published in the Cathedral of Lisbon. Shortly after, a general recantation of Conversos occurred in front of the Church of the Hospitalers. As a result of the pardon, Inquisitional prisons in Lisbon, Evora, and Coimbra were emptied. The tribunals in Porto, Lamego, and Thomar were permanently closed. Approximately, 1,800 persons were released and set free.[11]

The Inquisition eventually resumed its operations. Conversos did experience a short lull from Inquisitional activity during the reign of King Sebastian. King Sebastian allowed Conversos, upon the receipt of 225,000 ducats, to leave the country. He also released Conversos from

---

different Christian states and are protected with especial privileges, which we formerly did not dare to expect. This, Sire, is our attitude." cited in Singer, Isidore; Adler, Cyrus; (eds.) The Jewish Encyclopedia, "Inquisition: called also Sanctum Officium or Holy Office." Last modified 1904. Accessed January 2, 2013.

[11] Singer, Isidore; Adler, Cyrus; (eds.) The Jewish Encyclopedia, "Inquisition: called also Sanctum Officium or Holy Office." Last modified 1904. Accessed January 2, 2013.

confiscation of their property for ten years. The Inquisition continued its operations and intensified them during the direction of Cardinal Henrique.

The General Pardon of 1604

On August 3, 1603, an *auto da fé* was held on the Praça Ribeiro in Lisbon, with the Spanish viceroy in attendance. Among those sentenced to die, was the Franciscan Diego de la Assencion. After reading the Bible, he had concluded that he should embrace Judaism. Thomar Barocas was among those who were burned.

Conversos once again tried limiting the Inquisition's authority. A year later after receiving a substantial bribe, Philip II approached Pope Clement VIII on behalf of the Conversos. The Pope agreed and issued a bull on August 23, 1604, which granted a general pardon. The edict was rather timely. As soon as the declaration reached Lisbon, 155 persons who had been indicted were released on January 16, 1605.

Under Philip IV, however, the cities of Lisbon, Evora, and Coimbra held at least one *auto da fé* every year. One notable *auto da fé* occurred in Lisbon on May 5, 1624. A deacon, named Antonio Homom condemned to the stake had preached in a secret synagogue in Lisbon. In 1629, the *autos da fé* held in Evora on April 1 and in Lisbon on September 2, 1629. A law was passed November 17 of that year allowing Conversos to emigrate without interference.

The Inquisition under the Reign of John IV

The Kingdom of Portugal regained its independence from Spain in 1640. Under the reign of King John IV, Conversos sought once again to limit if not end Inquisitional activity. Whether King John IV was in fact opposed by the grand inquisitor Francisco da Costa, or in fact decided against suspending the tribunal is unclear. The plight of Conversos subjected to Inquisitional authority continued.

On April 2, 1642, two exceptionally wealthy Conversos accused of practicing Judaism were executed in the presence of the Queen. In December 1647, Isaac de Castro Tartas, a philosopher, and five other Conversos were executed. An additional 60 persons were sentenced to life-long imprisonment or other punishments.

On December 1, 1652, the Portuguese consul-general and author Manuel Fernandes de Villa-Real was executed in Lisbon. On December 15, 1658, 90 Conversos appeared at an *auto da fé*. 6 of them were burned. They were accused of observing Jewish holidays and abstaining from swine's flesh.

Attempts to Restrain the Tribunal

Manuel Fernandes successfully obtained the consenting opinions of theologians and the Jesuits at the University of Coimbra and other colleges in 1673. The scholars spoke favorably of the Conversos. With the consent of the prince regent, Manuel Fernandes submitted the request to the Pope. The Conversos also sent a representative to Rome. They selected Francisco de Azevedo who described the cruel process of the Inquisition. Pope Clement X issued a bull on October 3, 1674, which ended Portuguese Inquisitional activity. It also prohibited any further conviction or confiscation of property.

In a repeat of previous events, when the bull was announced through the papal nuncio in Lisbon, it met with tremendous opposition from the inquisitors as well as a large segment of the Cortes. The Cortes urged the prince regent Pedro to suppress the pretensions of the Conversos. The authority of the Inquisition continued unimpeded.

Tension broke out between the papal nuncio, the Inquisitional authorities, and the royal court. The new inquisitor-general Verissimo de Alemcastro, appointed by Pope Innocent XI, Clement's successor, refused to comply with the papal command. The Pope ordered the nuncio to announce the bull of October 3, 1674, and ordered the inquisitor-general to turn over to the nuncio within ten days all tribunal documents. In the end, the Inquisition resumed its activity on the strength of a new bull issued on August 22, 1681. On May 10, 1682, the first of the new string of *autos da fé* representing the largest in the history of the Portuguese Inquisition began. On August 5, 1683, a law was enacted which

called for children of seven years and up to be taken away from the pa r-
ents if they latter had appeared before the tribunal. [12]

The Portuguese Inquisition in the Eighteenth Century

The Portuguese courts continued to operate in the eighteenth century, albeit at a lower intensity. Nevertheless, Conversos accused of practicing Judaism continued to be burned. *Autos* were held in Lisbon, Evora, and Coimbra in 1701, 1704, and in the subsequent years. In Lisbon, on September 6, 1705, 60 persons were accused of practicing Judaism. This *auto da fé* was characterized by the polemic of Bishop of Cranganor against Judaism. On June 30, 1706, six more Ju daizers were burned in Lisbon. The continued focus on Judaism is highlighted by the *auto da fé* held on July 9, 1713, in Lisbon. The Inquisitor Francisco Pedroso delivered a speech, which also appeared in print, which railed against Jewish infidelity.

On June 17, 1718, the tribunal in Coimbra condemned more than 60 Conversos, all of them from Braganza. Among them, Manuel Rodriguez de Carvalho and Isabella Mendes were accused of desecrating the host and were strangled and then burned. 13 On March 14, 1723, an apothecary from Braganza, Francisco Diaz, was also burned in Coimbra. On September 1, 1739, 4 men and 8 women were executed, and 35 other Judaizers were sentenced to life imprisonment.

King Joseph severely hindered the authority of the Inquisition. In 1751, he declared that before any trial commenced the prosecutors of the tribunal were to notify the accused of the charges against them. The names of the witnesses were to be disclosed. The accused were free to choose their counsel, and no verdict could be made without the approval of the government. No further *autos da fé* were allowed. Despite the crippling of its authority, the Inquisition was not completely abolished until March 31, 1821.

---

[12] Singer, Isidore; Adler, Cyrus; (eds.) The Jewish Encyclopedia, "Inquisi-tion: called also Sanctum Officium or Holy Office." Last modified 1904. Accessed January 2, 2013.

[13] Ibid.

The Portuguese Inquisition and Portuguese Colonies

The Portuguese Inquisition operated throughout the vast holdings of Portuguese overseas empire. The distances of this far-flung empire and the financial opportunities drew many Conversos to seek protection there. The headquarters of the overseas Portuguese Inquisition was based in Goa, in South India. Archbishop Gaspar de Leaõ, the first Grand Inquisitor, issued a public statement "to the people of Israel" on September 29, 1565. All Conversos found in the Portuguese colonies or on ships bound there were to be sent back to Portugal. If no ship was available, they were taken to Goa and held in prison there until a ship set sail for Portugal. A critical area of Converso activity was Brazil, though Inquisitional activity began rather late.

At the *auto da fé* held in Lisbon on December 15, 1649, 5 Judaizers from Pernambuco were burned. In Rio de Janeiro the Inquisition began its harassment of Conversos in 1702 under the term of Bishop Francisco da S. Jeronimo of Evora as governor.

The Inquisition in Rome

In direct opposition to the work of the Spanish and Portuguese Inquisitions, Pope Paul III initially sheltered the Spanish and Portuguese Conversos and permitted them to stay in Rome. In April 1542, he established the Congregatio Sancti Officii, which consisted of six cardinals. On September 4, 1542, the Franciscan Cornelio of Montalcino who had adopted Judaism was burned in Rome by papal decree. In contrast to Pope Paul III, Pietro Caraffa, Pope Paul IV moved to make the Italian Inquisition emulate its Spanish counterpart.

On April 30, 1556, he ordered that all Jews or Conversos arriving from Portugal be arrested and burned without delay. In May 1556, 24 persons were executed.[14]

---

[14] The executed included Simon ibn Menahem, Joseph Oheb, Joseph Papo, Abraham Cohen, Samuel Guascon, Abraham Falcon, and Abraham d'España, together with Solomon Yaḥya Jacob Mozo, Moses Pazo, Solomon Pinto, Solomon Aguades, Abraham Lobo, David Reuben, and Donna Majora were burned at Ancona. Ibid.

A riot broke out in Rome after the death of Pope Paul IV. The tribunal's headquarters were attacked. Documents were burned, and the prisons opened by force. Despite this, Pope Pius V strengthened the Inquisition while Pope Gregory XI gave it new jurisdiction over Jews. On February 9, 1583, Joseph Saralbo who had been born in Portugal and openly returned to Judaism was executed in Ferrara. The Inquisition continued its operations under Pope Paul V, Pope Gregory XV, and Pope Clement XI, but its focus on Jews and Conversos was nominal.Palermo served as the center of the Inquisition in Sicily but was now under the jurisdiction of the inquisitor-general of Spain. More than 200 persons were burned during the Sicilian Inquisition's reign. An additional 279 were burned in effigy, while another 300 individuals were subjected to a variety of lesser punishments. On March 30, 1782, Ferdinand IV abolished the Inquisition.

CHAPTER 8

Menasseh Ben Israel and the Inquisition

It is helpful to review a few sample cases to understand the trauma that individuals faced when arrested by the Inquisition. The information related by the remarkable Menasseh Ben Israel, who eventually served as a rabbi in the Amsterdam community, is particularly interesting. Menasseh was born in 1604. His Portuguese name was Manoel Dias Soeiro. His parents had been arrested by the Inquisition and left Lisbon shortly before Menasseh's birth. They eventually reached Amsterdam, the site of the growing community composed of former Conversos. Manasseh was brought up under Rabbi Isaac Uzziel of Fez. Rabbi Uzziel died in 1620 and was succeeded by Menasseh. Menasseh became a prominent printer, diplomat, writer, and rabbi.[1] He was instrumental in the return of Jews to

---

[1] Rabbi Menasseh Ben Israel authored a number of works including the practical guide for Conversos titled *Thesouro dos dinim que o povo de Israel e obrigado saber e observer*. Miriam Bodian, "Hebrews of the Portuguese Nation: The Ambiguous Boundaries of Self-Definition," Jewish Social Studies, New Series, Vol. 15, No. 1, Sephardi Identities (2008): 78-79.

England and also served as one of the first rabbis in the New World.[2]

Menasseh ben Israel related the following description of his father to Dr. Joan van Beverwijck on March 1, 1639.

"My father Joseph ben Israel, of pious memory, was deprived of all his property by the Hispanic Inquisition because he was a Jew. After having been three times subjected to cruel tortures and having lost his bodily health, he secretly betook himself to these Provinces, together with my mother, Rachele Soeira..."[3]

---

[2] Despite his accomplishments, Noah Rosenbloom argues that Menasseh Ben Israel was the least influential rabbi of the Amsterdam Sephardic community. He was certainly the lowest paid and on various occasions it appears he was slighted publicly despite his rabbinic credentials. To illustrate the rather low esteem in which he was held, Rosenbloom points to an incident in 1640, in which after objecting to the disparagement of his brother in law, and he was excommunicated and fined almost half his salary. Noah H. Rosenbloom, "Menasseh Ben Israel and the Eternality of Punishment Issue," Proceedings of the American Academy for Jewish Research, Vol. 60 (1994): 243-244.

[3] H.P. Salomon, "The Portuguese Background of Menasseh Ben Israel's Parents as Revealed through the Inquisitorial Archives at Lisbon," Studia Rosenthaliana, Vol. 17, No. 2 (1983): 105.

Inquisition Torture Chamber by Benard Picard

In his work Esperanca de Israel, Menasseh ben Israel record-ed the following story told to him by his father. "…in the city of Lisbon, a certain Moor had an hourglass filled with this sand (i.e. from the river Sabbation) and in order to defame the New Christians by equating them with Jews, used to pass through the Rua Nova, where they had their shops, on Friday toward nightfall, saying: 'shut your shops, Jews, for the Sabbath has already come.'"

Menasseh's father was known as Gaspar Rodrigues Nunes in Amsterdam and as Joseph ben Israel in the synagogue.[4] The Inquisition had arrested Gaspar as a result of the denunciation against him made by his wife, Felipa Rodrigues. Felipa had been arrested on October 13, 1591, and Gaspar was arrested on the 29th of October. Under torture, she confessed to having ob-

---

[4] Ibid., 106-107.

served Jewish fasts with her husband shortly after their marriage 12 years before.

She also implicated her aunt, Isabel Alvares, for having fasted decades before. On November 5th, 1593, Gaspar, Felipa, and Isabel were brought to the inquisitorial prison. Gaspar's father had been arrested in 1591 and remained in prison when his son was arrested.[5] Gaspar was interrogated multiple times and countered the charges of Judaizing by appealing to the fact that he was friends with different Old Christians. He named three Old Christians friends as character witnesses.

Despite this claim, he remained in prison until in 1596 and even argued that his wife was vindictive against him due to his treatment of her. Finally, on August 28th, 1596, despite the fact that denial of guilt typically led to a death sentence, Gaspar was to be freed after being subjected to one and a half stretches of the rack. If he withstood the torture without confessing, he would be released upon his abjuration at an *auto de fé*.

Menasseh Ben Israel

---

[5] Ibid., 108.

Unfortunately for Gaspar, his wife's aunt Isabel Alvares broke down when faced with the prospect of torture and implicated Gaspar as well. Like her niece, she claimed to have observed a fast with Gaspar twenty years earlier. Gaspar was confronted with another allegation, and his trial was reopened, and Gaspar was faced with the prospect of discounting the testimony against him.[6]

In the end, Gaspar underwent torture a third time. On December 16, 1596, he was broken and asked for the torture to stop to allow him to confess his sins.

"...he was a Jew and had believed in the Law of Moses for the last sixteen or seventeen years. He had obtained this belief from his stepmother Mor Rodrigues in his father's house on the Nail arcade and had held to it up to the time of his present confession. Fifteen or sixteen years ago he had married at Elvas his wife Felipa Rodrigues, the niece of his stepmother More Rodrigues and had observed Jewish fasts with her there. Thirteen or fourteen years ago he moved back from Elvas to Lisbon where he again took up residence on the Nail Arcade. At around that time, his wife's aunt, Isabel Alvares, the wife of Joao Moreno who had been in Peru for at least eight or more years, came to visit his wife and discussed Judaism with her. Four or five years ago he visited at the house of Ines Dias. She was the wife of Fernando Alvares, the confectioner, and they all discussed Judaism. Ten years ago his wife's Castilian first cousin Felipa Rodrigues, daughter of his wife's brother Alvaro Fernandes who also had a nail shop on the Nail Arcade, came to visit his wife and discussed Judaism.

The Inquisition afterward arrested the other Felipa Rodrigues, appeared at an *auto-de-fe* in a sabenito and he

---

[6] Ibid., 109-111.

never saw her again. Nine years ago Maria Alvares, another first cousin of his wife, the sister of Castilian Felipa Rodrigues, came to their house and discussed Judaism. She too suffered Inquisitorial arrest, paraded at an auto-de-fe in sanbenito, and he never saw her since. Twelve years ago his first cousin Manuel Dias, now aged...”[7]

Of the 36 men and 54 women condemned to different sentences at the *auto de fé* on February 23, 1597, several were founders of the Portuguese community in Amsterdam. After being arrested by the Inquisition, Felipa Rodrigues II began her confessions on August 1, 1591. She related that her aunt Maria Lopes the wife of Alfonso Rodrigues d'Elvas had taught her a "Jewish prayer." The prayer was a combination of Psalm 90, Psalm 17, and the third verse of Psalm 91: It read: "A fermosura de Adonay noso Dio, Feitos de nostras manos, Compensa sobre nos, O Senhor no livrara do laco de encantamento..."

Felipa Rodrigues was transferred from her original cell into another cell which had small holes allowing the Inquisitors to keep tabs on her activities. She was kept there with another prisoner named Beatris Mendes. Mendes had confessed that Felipa had observed fasts on Mondays, Tuesdays, Wednesdays, and Fridays. She also noted that Felipa had recited the following prayer,

"My God, the soul which Thou has given me, is clean; Thou hast created it in me; Thou has breathed it into me; Thou art ready to take it from me..."[8]

The guards assigned to watch Felipa also reported that she had thrown pork through the window and soup into the urinary. She had also failed to cross herself when she awoke from bed. Felipa eventually confessed on November 20th that her aunt had taught her to recite the prayer derived from the Elohai neshamah

---

[7] Ibid., 112.
[8] Ibid., 118.

when fasting and to do so while standing with her palms stretched out. She eventually confessed to knowing other Jewish prayers which she stated her aunt, Lianor Alvares had taught her.[9] A translation of one of the prayers she admitted to knowing are as follows and betrays a measure of memorization and some Jewish elements which are derived from various biblical passages.

"O my God, O my LORD, King of Kings, LORD of Hosts, Thou art my God forever. Thou art the fortress of my life and art the all of my soul and the support of my house. Thou art the One whose years have no end, and therefore I confess myself to Thee to sing Thy praise, and my life is in Thy hands, and my soul is in Thy power and Thy miracles and good deeds and marvels and acts of loving-kindness Thou workest at all hours for me. Do not forsake nor undo that which Thou hast created in Thy holy image. Thou art God of truth, we all hope in Thee. Free us LORD of eternities and of steps from the world as Thou hast freed Abraham the Patriarch from the power of the five kings and Joseph from chains and Daniel from the lions. In the same way pray, free Thou me and all that I dearly love. Illuminate O LORD my heart with Thy brilliance, give me LORD alms from Thy hand and not from the hand of man whose gifts are grudging and humiliating. Keep me LORD from the fire of hell and illuminate me with Thy Peace and put Thy good over me, my LORD and Adonai."[10]

During her confession to the Inquisitors, Felipa notes that she never practiced any other Jewish ceremonies but had 5 or 6 years earlier declared her belief in the Law of Moses. She had done this along with her cousin Felipa Rodrigues. What this re-

---

[9] Ibid., 119, 121.
[10] Ibid., 122.

flects is the essential idea that adherence to Judaism was evidenced by a declaration of faith akin to the Christian understanding of belief. She was confronted with the possibility of further torture which led her to implicate others.

Regarding the Inquisitional trial of Alvaro Rodrigues, the paternal grandfather of Menasseh Ben Israel, we learn more relating to the perception of the critical elements identified with Jewish belief. The Inquisition had arrested Rodrigues after being denounced by this daughter who had been detained earlier in 1591. His daughter, Branca declared that 22 years earlier, at the age of 14, her father had revealed the following to her: "…to believe in one sole God who created heaven and earth, land, sea and sands and to commend herself to Him and to believe only in Him and to keep the Sabbaths for God rested on them and worked all the other days of the week, creating heaven and earth, and only on the Sabbath did He rest, and to believe only in the Law of Moses and keep it, for that very law was maintained by her forefathers who were the Jews of former times, and only this her father told her on just this one occasion."[11]

---

[11] Ibid., 123, 127.

CHAPTER 9

Debating the Inquisition

One of the first analyses of the Inquisition's records was conducted in 1811 by Juan Antonio Llorente. Llorente was employed by the Holy Office and had unfettered access to tribunal records. His work titled Historia Crit ica de la Inquisicion en Espana argued that greed was the motivating factor behind the work of the Inquisition, an idea that in altered form would be adopted by later scholars.[1] He was so certain that the confiscation of property was the ultimate goal of the Inquisition that he wrote the following:

"Facts prove beyond a doubt, that the extirpation of Judaism was not the real cause, but the pretext, for the establishment of the Inquisition by King Ferdinand V. The true

---

[1] The Jewishness of the Conversos and consequently the authenticity of the testimonies recorded by the Inquisition has come under considerable scrutiny in recent decades. A conflict exists between the views of Yitzhak Baer and Haim Beinart and those of Benzion Netanyahu and Norman Roth. Baer and Beinart considered the conversion of Jews as largely as conversions under compulsion. Roth and Netanyahu viewed most conversions as voluntary, or simply the product of economic or cultural distress

motive was to carry on a vigorous system of confiscation against the Jews."[2]

Dom Diego da Annunciacao Justiano

Llorente's views were partly buttressed by a cleric of the 17th and 18th centuries, Dom Diego da Annunciacao Justiano (1654-1713). Dom Diego preached at *autos da fé* in Portugal. He supported the contention that Judaizing was not the real motivation behind the Inquisition, or at least not the only one.[3]

Dom Diego was familiar with the Portuguese Inquisition. The Portuguese Inquisition lessened in ferocity after 1705, but activity was sporadic. From 1720 to 1725, ninety or so persons were executed.[4] As a consequence, from 1720 until 1733 approximately 1,500 Converso immigrants arrived in London directly.[5]

A former New Christian joined Dom Diego's incredulity regarding Judaizing. The latter raised the question regarding the

---

[2] Ibid. 10-11.

[3] In 1705, Dom Diego stated: "Miserable relics of Judaism! Unhappy fragments of the synagogue! Last remains of Judea! Scandal of the Catholics and testable objects of scorn to the Jews for you are so ignorant that you cannot even observe the vey law under which you live..." H.P. Salomon, "New Light on the Portuguese Inquisition: The Second Reply to the Archbishop of Cranganor," Studia Rosenthaliana, Vol. 5 No. 2 (1971): 178.

[4] Joseph Perez also points to the memoirs of the Mexican monk Servando Teresa de Mier. Servano noted in his memoirs in 1801 of New Christians in Bayonne who had recently been circumcised. Joseph Perez, *The Spanish Inquisition: A History* (London: Profile Books, 2006), 40.

[5] H.P. Salomon, "New Light on the Portuguese Inquisition: The Second Reply to the Archbishop of Cranganor," Studia Rosenthaliana, Vol. 5 No. 2 (1971): 182.

role the Inquisition played in stirring up Crypto-Jewish practices. He wrote,

"...having set up all these Courts and Officials only to
prevent God's Law from being kept and to blot out its
memory as well as the whole Jewish people, the Inquisition itself becomes its greatest teacher. It increases the
number of Jews by making them keepers of the Law of
which they were ignorant...God permits the Jews to learn
the Holy Law from the very rigor with which they are
punished and allow the Officers who prohibit it to become its teachers and to actually teach it...thus the very
inquisitors end up by teaching it more efficiently than if it
were a subject in public schools and notwithstanding the
Inquisition's great secrecy men, women and children
come to know it. Thus they teach the Law which they
wish to destroy...for one this is sure: if there were no Inquisitions, by this time, in Portugal and Spain, there
would no longer be any Jews. We owe the Inquisition the
Law's survival as well as the reputation of all being Jews
which Spaniards and Portuguese have throughout the
world..."[6]

Dom argued that the confessions to Jewish observances by
those arrested by the Inquisitors were simply ruses to secure release. However, as we have seen through the brief review of the
Inquisitional cases of Menasseh Ben Israel and his family, confessions did, in fact, lead to the disclosure of actual practices. A
New Christian author writing in reply to Dom Diego states:

"...because telling the truth in this Inquisitional Court is
the most foolhardy and the stupidest thing you can do;
because in it whoever lies most has the best chance of
getting out. This is what they call the best confession because by these lies they bring in more false

---

[6] Ibid., 184.

witnesses…this, neither more nor less is what the Tribunal does, proclaiming merciful deeds and calling is…"[7]
Dom also states the following:

"… the worst of the matter is that among every hundred of these unfortunates at the very most ten are guilty and the other ninety just as Catholic and papist as the Inquisitors who tyrannize them are themselves. The unfortunates are so firm and constant in the Faith that when the rope is already around their neck, with their last breath, they proclaim that they are Christians and that they die believing in Christ, but this the Holy Piety of these Officials dismisses as being a sham…"[8]

What Dom Diego failed to address is how he was so certain that those accused were innocent. Individuals claiming to be faithful Christians till the end may have believed that continuing to argue the former to receive mercy from the Inquisitors.

Faced with death, some may have chosen to die as martyrs, but when confronted with the option of the garrote versus burning alive, many may have opted to choose the path that led to them to an easier passing. The counter effects of the Inquisition were as follows according to the author: "…they say it is in order to make Christians out of Jews, but what they are in fact doing is making Jews of Christians…"[9] A Converso author who has returned to Judaism argues that the real source of the Inquisition's persecution was not because Conversos have kept the Torah, but quite the opposite.

"…the Inquisitional Tribunal claims that it arrests Jews for being guilty of keeping God's Law, but this is deceit; the crime for which they catch us and punish us so

---

[7] Ibid., 184-185.

[8] H.P. Salomon, "New Light on the Portuguese Inquisition: The Second Reply to the Archbishop of Cranganor," Studia Rosenthaliana, Vol. 5 No. 2 (1971): 185.

[9] Ibid., 185.

tyrannically is that of not having kept it…and in order to preserve it in Portugal and Spain, God maintained these tribunals in these Kingdoms, and instead of making the Jews Christians, He is making the Christians Jews, that's the truth…"[10]

Antonio Vieira, a Portuguese Jesuit philosopher, wrote to Pope Innocent XI and argued that the Inquisitional tactics had counter effects: "They want to help one Old Christian, and they make two hundred New Christians. Just as coins are stamped in the Royal Mint so in this miserable kingdom we have factories for minting Jews; if before they were not known as such [i.e. New Christians] here, they imprint them with the stamp and they are marked with crosses so that all the world will know them. This is new arithmetic while intending to subtract actually multiplies."[11] Antonio Vieira had the unique position to comment since the Inquisition arrested him and accused of heresy.

A review of his controversial positions, however, may actual reveal that the Inquisition was focused on those elements which characterized Jewish or Jewish learning beliefs or observances. Over the course of his life, Vieira maintained extensive relationships with Jews and New Christians. Vieira lived in the Bahia, the colonial capital of the Portuguese colony in Brazil. He lived there until 1618 when a second Visitor of the Inquisition arrived. There he had intimate contact with New Christians who had settled there.

Vieira maintained close relationships with New Christians there and was friendly with a very successful New Christian merchant and financier named Duarta da Silva. Silva was influential in the struggle against Spanish rule for the return of the House of Braganza. Following the restoration of Portuguese in-

---

[10] Ibid., 186. Anita Novinsky, "Padre Antonio Vieiera, The Inquisition, and the Jews," Jewish History Vol. 6, Nos. 1-3 (1992):152, 157.

[11] Ibid., 157.

dependence, Vieira served the restored monarchy as an adviser. His contacts and relationships with Jews of Portuguese extraction made him adopt pro-New Christian position. He believed it was critical for Portugal to form alliances with the principal New Christian financiers.

In 1643, he urged that New Christians who had fled Portugal be granted amnesty. He also argued they should be exempted from paying taxes. The distinctions between Old and New Christians should be eliminated as well.[12] He claimed that intermarriage between Old Christians and New Christians should be encouraged and even requested that the Pope grant a pardon to Judaizers.[13] Vieira positive disposition towards Jews was apparently influenced by his reading of and his interpretation of the Old Testament as well as various works banned by the Index.

According to Anita Novinsky, Jewish history and Jewish thought permeate his letters and his sermons. That fact was a key factor that led to his arrest.[14] All in all, it does not appear to have been an unreasonable assumption by the Inquisition. Novinsky states:

"If we consider the political history of Portugal during the period of the Restoration, we will understand the reasons why Vieira's attitudes and influence in the Court of D. Joao Iv disturbed the ministers of the Holy Office, who perceived in them the potential enemy hidden in the personality of the Jesuit. Vieira's imprisonment by the Inquisition is linked to his political message, to his social criticism, and to his writings on behalf of New Christians. In his trial, he was accused of Judaism, sacrilege, blas-

---

[12] Anita Novinsky, "Padre Antonio Vieiera, The Inquisition, and the Jews," Jewish History Vol. 6, Nos. 1-3 (1992): 151.

[13] Ibid., 152.

[14] Ibid., 152.

phemy, and of having defended ideas impregnated with Jewish heresy, Vieira recanted. But even after he was acquitted, he did not abandon his millenarian ideas, nor his defense of the Jewish cause."[15]

While some may argue that the accusation of Judaizing was false, it highlights the Inquisition's focus on the very existence of pro-Jewish sentiment which they believed to be a justifiable marker of Jewish identity. All in all, it does not appear to have been an unreasonable assumption. The New Christian author continues by stating,

Martha Krow-Lucal also provides an example of the Inquisition's genuine concern over crypto-Judaism and their willingness to forgo financial gain to prove a point. A Majorca Converso named Pedro Onofre Cortes owned a piece of land which he used as a garden. The garden was frequented by other Conversos to celebrate Jewish holidays. He was arrested in 1679 and his property confiscated. His garden was seized, plowed under, and sowed with salt. A plaque was placed in the middle of the former garden which read as follows:

"Year 1679 this garden was demolished and sowed with salt by order of the Inquisition because the Law of Moses was taught in it. None may break or take away this stone at any time, under pain of excommunication." [16]

The sign posted remained until the nineteenth century. It is for Krow-Lucal proof that there were more pressing issues at stake for the Inquisition that in just seizing property.

"If the Inquisition had simply been interested in economic gain, it could have taken the land for its own use, or rented it out. To destroy for generations a fertile piece of land- on an island!- by sowing it with salt is a strong

---

[15] Ibid., 152.

[16] Angela Selke, *Los Chuetas y La Inquisicion* (Madrid: Taurus, 1972), 81.

symbolic statement that indicates another type of concern."[17]

While confiscations could prove lucrative depending on the individual on trial, the critical issue that stands against such a pure motivation is the extent to which the tribunals meticulously recorded their work. The arrangement regarding the division of confiscated property saw one-third go to the Holy Office; one-third go to the local tribunal and one-third to the royal court. Were confiscation the only aim, the very purpose or benefit of such detailed trial accounts seems dubious. As Anne D'Abrera notes:

"It is generally understood that the records of the Holy Office were classified information which were for the eyes of the inquisitors only, and it, therefore, seems absurd that those working for the Holy Office should conspire together to censor documents that only they could read."[18]

In short, were economic gain the only concern, a much more efficient way to seize such wealth could certainly have been arranged. Nevertheless, because of Despite Llorente's belief in the ulterior motives of the Inquisition, he along with a number of other historians including the devout traditional Catholic Marcelino Menendez Pelayo, and perhaps the most famous chronicler of the Inquisition Charles Lea, indeed believed that a significant crypto-Jewish movement did, in fact, exist in the 15th and 16th centuries which in short from the perspective of the Church justified the creation of the Inquisition. [19]

---

[17] Martha G. Krow-Lucal, "Marginalizing History: Observations on the Origins of the Inquisition in Fifteenth-Century Spain by B. Netanyahu." Judaism Volume 46 Issue, (1997): 57.

[18] Anna Ysabel D'Abrera, *The Tribunal of Zaragoza and Crypto-Judaism 1484-1515* (Turnhout: Brepols Publishers, 2008), 191.

[19] Ibid., 12.

THE RISE OF THE INQUISITION

The Perspective of Yitzhak Baer and Haim Beinart

Anna D' Abrera notes that as early as 1820, the tribunal's archives in Galicia, Logrono, and Valladolid had vanished. Those of Valencia, Majorca, and Seville were also heavily compromised. The records of the Central Council of the Inquisition known as the Suprema fared better. The collections of Toledo, Cuenca, Ciudad Real, Valencia, and Zaragoza conserved elements intact.[20] Correspondingly, when speaking of the Inquisition and its actions, we must then understand that all records are not available and we are operating with incomplete facts.

The preeminent historian of Iberian Jewish history, Yitzhak Baer related his view of the ongoing interaction and ties between Jews and Conversos.

"Conversos and Jews were one people, united by bonds of religion, destiny and messianic hope, which in Spain took on a unique coloration typical of the people and the country...The confession and testimonies contained in these records (of the Inquisition) breathe a nostalgic yearning for the national homeland, both earthly and heavenly- a yearning for all things, great and small, sanctified by the national tradition, and for something even greater, which had created the people and maintained in life."[21]

---

[20] Ibid., 9-10.

[21] Yitzhak Baer, *A History of the Jews in Christian Spain Volume 2* (Philadelphia: Jewish Publication Society, 1961), 424-425. The Inquisition as well as Spanish society linked Jewish attributes to Conversos. Regarding the Inquisition, Starr-LeBeau writes "The Holy office recognized instinct for self-preservation, as had inquisitorial and secular courts for centuries; here it became joined to stereotypes of shifty dishonest New Christians that had their origins in stereotypes of Jews." Gretchen D. Starr-LeBeau, *In the Shadow of the Virgin: Inquisitors,*

For Haim Beinart, Jews and Conversos shared the same fate. As D'Abrera describes, Beinart and Baer were both dedicated to the belief that the available records represented irrefutable evidence of the Conversos' continuing adherence to Judaism.[22] This shared destiny included persecution, violence, expulsion and martyrdom.

For Beinart, Conversos who returned to Judaism or even expressed their desire to do so could expect to be welcome without reservation by their Jewish compatriots everywhere.[23] For Beinart, the relationship between Jews and their Converso brethren was clear cut and required little elaboration.

Benzion Netanyahu's and Norman Roth's Challenge

While Yitzhak Baer and Haim Beinart accepted the Inquisitional records as reliable sources, Ben Zion Netanyahu claimed that the Inquisitional records were unreliable at best, and in the case of Norman Roth, outright fiction. The centrality of such a perspective relies on two key issues. The first is the premise that the Inquisitional goals were not the eradication of Judaizing among Conversos, but rather the destruction of this social-economic class as a whole. The second is the view that since the overwhelming majority of Conversos were sincere Christians, Inquisitional charges must necessary be false.

"Marrano Christianization had been steadily advancing for three generations (from 1391 on), so that at the beginning of the 1480s, when the Spanish Inquisition was

---

Friars, and Conversos in Guadalupe, Spain (Princeton, Princeton University Press, 2003), 154.

[22] Anna Ysabel D'Abrera, *The Tribunal of Zaragoza and Crypto-Judaism 1484-1515* (Brepols Publishers, Turnhout, 2008), 12.

[23] Haim Beinart points to the work of S. Assaf, *The Tents of Jacob, Jerusalem*, 1944, 145-180 reviewing rabbinic responsa on the issue.

established, virtually all Jewish authorities in Spain and elsewhere regarded the mass of the Marranos as renegades-that is as apostates or Gentiles. By any these definitions, they were Christians and in no way Judaizers or crypto-Jews."[24]

The tribunals were therefore unreliable, and for Norman Roth, the litany of Jewish practices which in fact often reappear in various trials is not, in fact, reflective of the typical elements of Jewish faith that Conversos would naturally have continued to maintain, but rather the inability of the Inquisition to conjure up better false charges. Roth unequivocally states:"There is no doubt whatever that in the overwhelming majority, nearly all of these accusations are totally false."[25]

Countering such a view, Yosef Hayim Yerushalmi wrote: "To regard [Inquisitorial dossiers] as a means of spreading the fiction of crypto-Judaism for propaganda purposes presents a strange dilemma. It would mean that, in recording the details of Judaizing practices into the dossiers of the accused, the inquisitors were purposely transcribing a tissue of lies for the perusal of other inquisitors who were engaged in the same conspiracy. But this is manifestly absurd."[26]

Netanyahu was willing to admit limited rare cases of Crypto-Judaism. Even then, he blamed the Inquisition for the resurgence of Judaic practices among Conversos he assumed was assimilated. Any vestiges of Jewish identity "would have, in all likelihood, soon faded into nothingness, had not the process of

---

[24] Benzion Netanyahu, *The Marranos of Spain: From the Late 14th to the Early 16th Century, According to Contemporary Hebrew Sources* (Ithaca: Cornell University Press, 1999), xviii.

[25] Norman Roth, *Conversos, Inquisition, and the Expulsion of the Jews from Spain,* (Madison: University of Wisconsin, Press, 1995), 40.

[26] Yosef Hayim Yerushalmi, *From Spanish Court to Venetian Ghetto* (Seattle: University of Washington Press, 1981), 23.

assimilation been violently interfered with by the repellent and bewildering actions of the Inquisitional and that thus it was due to the Inquisition itself that the dying Marranism in Spain was given a new lease on life."[27]

With the ability to in fact fabricate any charge against any individual, the destruction of the Converso social-economic class was an easy goal. The destruction of the Conversos was per Netanyahu anti-Semitic in nature as amply proven by the purity of blood laws which were eventually adopted. A primary contention is the repetitive character of the accusations recorded by Inquisitors (i.e. lighting Shabbat candles, avoiding pork, circumcision, etc.) which Roth argues is proof of the emptiness of the charges.

I would contend, however, that if American Jewry were ever to face a similar situation of persecution which resulted in mass conversions, the types of Jewish observances which would likely be practiced by those Jews determined to observe Judaism clandestinely would be eerily similar. This should not be so strange as they reflect the common observances identifiable to most Jews and non-Jews.

It is important to note that Yitzhak Baer, despite his overall disagreement with Netanyahu was willing to recognize the multifaceted nature of the Inquisitional procedure and its susceptibility to an agenda outside of suppressing Judaizing. Baer stated: "The Inquisition had usually taken pains, according to their rights to proceed in accordance with the rules of law and justice, demonstrating facts which were unquestionably correct and refraining from malicious libels. Now, however, they began to conduct a trial, from beginning to

---

[27] Benzion Netanyahu, *The Marranos of Spain: From the Late 14th to the Early 16th Century, According to Contemporary Hebrew Sources* (Ithaca: Cornell University Press, 1999), 3.

end on the basis of the vile slanders which emanated solely from the imaginations of medieval anti-Semites."[28]

However, as D'Abrera notes, Baer was capable of assessing individual tribunals instead of applying a blanket charge to all the tribunals.[29] Baer was willing to see the differences in how each court related to those on trial. In the case of the court at Valencia, Baer saw a more measured if not lenient approach if one can designate this as such in its prosecution of Conversos.[30] This was in comparison to the tribunal at Ciudad Real who Yitzhak Baer as intent on destroying Conversos with a comparable laxity in its procedural process which Baer designated as betraying ulterior motives.[31] Albert Sicroff argued that Netanyahu was in effect focused on one of two extremes of Converso life.

"Netanyahu has chosen to emphasize only one of the two poles between which Jewish opinion oscillated on the Marrano question, that which castigated the Marranos as apostates who were becoming increasingly assimilated into Christian society."[32]

Nor is it necessary to eliminate the religious characteristics Conversos possessed from the charge of anti-Semitism that Netanyahu and Roth so confidently see as the real motivation behind the Inquisition. As Angus Mackay notes, just like Jewish identity, anti-Semitism need not be singularly expressed in the form of racial hatred, but could just as easily encompass the re-

---

[28] Yitzhak Baer, *A History of the Jews in Christian Spain, Volume 2* (Philadelphia: Jewish Publication Society, 1961), 398.

[29] Anna Ysabel D'Abrera, *The Tribunal of Zaragoza and Crypto-Judaism 1484-1515* (Turnhout: Brepols Publishers, 2008), 152.

[30] Yitzhak Baer, *A History of the Jews in Christian Spain, Volume 2* (Philadelphia: Jewish Publication Society, 1961), 334.

[31] Ibid. 292.

[32] Martha G. Krow-Lucal, "Marginalizing History: Observations on the Origins of the Inquisition in Fifteenth-Century Spain by B. Netanyahu." *Judaism* Volume 46 Issue (1997): 48.

ligious practices that Conversos were accused of practicing as well as the social and economic rank many of them enjoyed.[33] Paradoxically, the very institution intent on once and for all ending Converso identity was, according to Netanyahu, responsible for breathing brief life into it.[34]

The inherent problem with Netanyahu's position, is as Martha Krow-Lucal notes, his sweeping generalizations about large heterogeneous groups. Netanyahu's depiction of the Conversos is that there were almost no Judaizers. The problem, however, lies in the fact that the overwhelming evidence of crypto-Jewish tradition has been demonstrated by both the Inquisition records that Netanyahu dismisses as well as the stream of Converso refugees to Jewish communities in North Africa, Europe, and the Ottoman Empire.[35]

In the end, the unacceptability of dismissing the majority of the Inquisitional documents as trustworthy is evident. With regards to the Inquisitional records, Yosef Yerushalmi states:

"To view the Inquisitors as involved in what amounts to a universal conspiracy of fabrication is to ignore the mentality of men of a bygone day and to flatter them with Machiavellian intentions and capabilities beyond their reach."[36]

As D'abrera notes, the complexity of actually carrying out such a conspiracy would necessitate the organization and or-

---

[33] Anna Ysabel D'Abrera, *The Tribunal of Zaragoza and Crypto-Judaism 1484-1515*, (Turnhout: Brepols Publishers, 2008), 14.

[34] Ibid. 17.

[35] Martha G. Krow-Lucal, "Marginalizing History: Observations on the Origins of the Inquisition in Fifteenth-Century Spain by B. Netanyahu," Judaism Volume 46 Issue (1997): 48.

[36] Yosef Haim Yerushalmi, *From Spanish Court to Italian Ghetto. Isaac Cardoso: A Study in Seventeenth Century Marranism and Jewish Apologetics* (New York & London: Columbia University Press, 1971), 24.

chestration of the Supreme Council, something for which evidence just does not exist. The countless number of witnesses, interrogations, and confessions which would serve as Netanyahu and especially Roth claim are fictional or dubious cannot be explained away without supporting evidence to the contrary.[37] As D'Abrera explains:

> "Netanyahu is of the opinion that any conclusions previously arrived at by scholars researching the Inquisition have been erroneous precisely because they have mistakenly chosen to consult its records. He believes that his fellow historians have been duped, themselves becoming victims of a vast conspiracy which took place among the Old Christians five hundred years ago."[38]

Burning at the Stake

Benzion Netanyahu's claim of anti-Semitism as a primary motivator should not, however, be ultimately dismissed. Researchers should remember the latent if not open anti-Semitism

---

[37] Anna Ysabel D'Abrera, *The Tribunal of Zaragoza and Crypto-Judaism 1484-1515* (Turnhout: Brepols Publishers, 2008), 195.

[38] Ibid. 195.

existent in many quarters of the Spanish-speaking world. The anti-Semitism, however, is most often intrinsically linked with anti-Judaism. Roth's obsession with extricating blame on either Ferdinand or Isabella is somewhat confusing. In this respect, Netanyahu is slightly more contemplative regarding the partici-pation of Ferdinand and Isabella in the expulsion order. Netan-yahu states:

> "The Spanish kings felt the rising tide of anti-Semitism, and rather than resist it; they decided to ride it. This is, in essence, what was behind the determination to establish-and uphold- the Spanish Inquisition."[39]

Hateful and destructive as it was, the individuals who led the Inquisition appear for all purposes to be genuinely and radically faithful to their religious agenda. While monetary benefits may have added energy to the motivation, we need not assume that they would have detracted from the commitment of the Inquis i-tors. The symbolic idea of the wealth of the wicked being appropriated to the faithful would certainly be in concert with what the Inquisitors envisioned as a holy mission. Stephen Haliczer writes:

> "I cannot accept [the] interpretation of the role of Valen-cia's inquisitors as the docile clients and ser vants of the Inquisitor-Generals who appointed them. Once in Valen-cia, the inquisitors were far from the reproving eye of the inquisitor-general or Suprema, and each man tended to interpret for himself the role of provincial inquisitor…the Inquisition in Valencia was founded at a supreme mo-ment of religious fanaticism and strong centralization."[40]

---

[39] Ibid. 16. Benzion Netanyahu, *Toward the Inquisition: Essays on Jewish and Converso History in Late Medieval Spain* (New York: Cornell University Press, 1997), 200.

[40] Stephen Haliczer, *Inquisition and Society in the Kingdom of Va-lencia, 1478-1834* (Berkley: University of California Press, 1990), 6.

Samuel Usque's Description of the Inquisition

For anyone looking to contextualize the activities of the Inquisition and diminish its severity in light of medieval events, the famous Converso author, Samuel Usque, describes the Inquisition as a horrific and deadly monster. Samuel Usque had undergone forced conversion and eventually escaped from Portugal in the 16th century. His description, however metaphorical, provides an insight into how the Inquisition was viewed by those who suffered under it.

"The king and queen sent to Rome for a wild monster, of such strange form and horrible mien that all Europe trembles at the mere mention of its name. Its body, and an amalgam of hard iron and deadly poison has an adamantine shell made of steel and covered with enormous scales. It rises in the air on a thousand wings with black and poisonous pinions, and it moves on the ground with a thousand pernicious and destructive feet. Its form is like both the awesome lions and the frightful serpents in the deserts of Africa. Its enormous teeth equal those of the most powerful elephants."[41]

According to Jose Faur, the purpose of the Inquisition was to pollute and perverse its victims.[42] The power of the Inquisition as Faur notes, enticed some Conversos to molest, persecute, and assail their fellow Conversos who continued to adhere to Jewish practices. As Faur relates, "There was something Machiavellian and perverse in the Christian practice of using former Jews to persecute other Jews, especially members of their own families."[43]

---

[41] Jose Faur, *In the Shadow of History: Jews and Conversos at the Dawn of Modernity* (New York: SUNY, 1992), 198.

[42] Ibid., 194.

[43] Ibid., 45.

Afterword

Despite its long reign, the Tribunal is nothing more than a historical institution for most people. The Inquisition seems little more than the vestiges of the pre-enlightenment era. In many ways, this assessment is correct.

For others, however, the Inquisition's legacy remains powerful. Hundreds if not thousands of individuals in the 20th and 21st century in North and South America as well as in Spain, Portugal, Italy, and other have received a family tradition that they are the descendants of Jews who converted to Christianity centuries ago.

Some of their ancestors may have even been victims of the Inquisition. Other individuals through genealogical research or DNA testing encounter a Jewish past rooted in the Iberian Peninsula that was previously unknown to them.

By itself, history cannot resolve questions of identity. It can, however, provide us with a framework to understand who we are as individuals and how we have reached a particular point in our existence.

Bibliography

Abrera, Anna Ysabel D. The Tribunal of Zaragoza and Crypto-Judaism, 1484-1515. Turnhout, Belgium: Brepols, 2008.

Adler, Cyrus, and Isidore Singer. "Inquisition." Jewish Encyclopedia. 1906. Accessed June 9, 2015. http://www.jewishencyclopedia.com/articles/8122-inquisition.

Adler, Cyrus, and Isidore Singer. "Apostasy and Apostates from Judaism." Jewish Encyclopedia. 1906. Accessed June 9, 2015. http://www.jewishencyclopedia.com/articles/1654-apostasy-and-apostates-from-judaism.

"Al-Taqiyya, Dissimulation Part I." Al Islam. Accessed June 2, 2015. http://www.al-islam.org/shiite-encyclopedia-ahlul-bayt-dilp-team/al-taqiyya-dissimulation-part-I.

Albert, Bat-Sheva. "Isidore of Seville: His Attitude Towards Judaism and His Impact on Early Medieval Canon Law." The Jewish Quarterly Review 80, no. 3-4 (1990): 207-20.

Alfassa, Shelomo. The Sephardic 'Anousim': The Forcibly Converted Jews of Spain and Portugal. New York: ISLC, 2010.

Alpert, Michael. Crypto-judaism and the Spanish Inquisition. Basingstoke, Hampshire: Palgrave, 2001.

Alter, Alexandra. "'Secret Jews' of the Spanish Inquisition." Derkeiler. August 6, 2005. Accessed March 30, 2015. http://newsgroups.derkeiler.com/Archive/Soc/soc.culture.cuba/2005-08/msg00977.html.

Altmann, Alexander. "Eternality of Punishment: A Theological Controversy within the Amsterdam Rabbinate in the Thirties of the Seventeenth Century." Proceedings of the American Academy for Jewish Research 40 (1972): 1-88.

Amital, Yehuda. "A Torah Perspective on the Status of Secular Jews Today." The Israel Koschitzky Virtual Beit Midrash. Accessed January 13, 2015. http://etzion.org.il/vbm/english/alei/2-2chilo.htm.

Amran, Rica. "Judíos Y Conversos En Las Crónicas De Los Reyes De Castilla (desde Finales Del Siglo XIV Hasta La Expulsión)." Espacio, Tiempo Y Forma Serie III, no. 9 (1996): 257-76.

Antine, Nissan. "Responsa Relating to the Conversos." Lecture, from Beth Sholom and Talmud Torah, Potomac, January 1, 2010.

Antonio Escudero, José. "Luis Vives Y La Inquisicion." Revista De La Inquisición : Intolerancia Y Derechos Humanos 13 (2009): 11-24.

Assis, Yom Tov. "The Jews of the Maghreb and Sepharad: A Case Study of Inter-communal Cultural Relations through the Ages." El Prezente 2 (2008): 11-30.

Baer, Yitzhak. A History of the Jews in Christian Spain. Vol. II. Philadelphia: Jewish Publication Society of America, 1961.

Barnai, Jacob. "Christian Messianism and the Portuguese Marranos: The Emergence of Sabbateanism in Smyrna." Jew History Jewish History 7, no. 2 (1993): 119-26.

Baron, Salo W. A Social and Religious History of the Jews. Vol. IV. Philadelphia: Jewish Publication Society, 1957.

Baron, Salo W. A Social and Religious History of the Jews. Vol. IX. New York: Columbia University Press, 1965.

Baron, Salo W. A Social and Religious History of the Jews. Vol. X. Philadelphia: Jewish Publication Society, 1965.

Baron, Salo W. A Social and Religious History of the Jews. Vol. XI. Philadelphia: Jewish Publication Society, 1967.

Baron, Salo W. A Social and Religious History of the Jews. Vol. XIII. Philadelphia: Jewish Publication Society, 1969.

Baxter Wolf, Kenneth. "Sentencia-Estatuto De Toledo, 1449." Texts in Translation. 2008. Accessed June 2, 2015. https://sites.google.com/site/canilup/toledo1449.

Beinart, Haim, and Yael Guiladi. Conversos on Trial: The Inquisition in Ciudad Real. Jerusalem: Magnes Press, Hebrew University, 1981.

Beinart, Haim. The Expulsion of the Jews from Spain. Oxford: Littman Library of Jewish Civilization, 2002.

Ben-Sasson, Menahem. "On the Jewish Identity of Forced Converts: A Study of Forced Conversion in the Almohade Period." Pe'amim 42 (1990): 16-37.

Ben-Shalom, Ram. "Between Official and Private Dispute: The Case of Christian Spain and Provence in the Late Middle Ages." AJS Review 27, no. 1, 23-71.

Ben-Shalom, Ram. "The Converso as Subversive: Jewish Traditions or Christian Libel?" Journal of Jewish Studies 50, no. 2 (1999): 259-83.

Ben-Shalom, Ram. "The Typology of the Converso in Isaac Abravanel's Biblical Exegesis." Jew History Jewish History 23, no. 3 (2009): 281-92.

Ben-Ur, Aviva. ""Fakelore" or Historically Overlooked Sub-Ethnic Group?" HNet Humanities and Social Sciences Online. 2010. Accessed June 9, 2015. http://www.h-net.org/reviews/showrev.php?id=29438.

Benveniste, Arthur. "Finding Our Lost Brothers and Sisters: The Crypto-Jews of Brazil." Western States Jewish History 29, no. 3 (1997): 103-09.

Benveniste, Henriette-Rika. "On the Language of Conversion: Visigothic Spain Revisited." Historein 6 (2006): 72-87.

Berenbaum, Michael, and Fred Skolnik, eds. "Isaac Ben Sheshet Perfet." Encyclopedia Judaica. 2nd ed. Vol. 10. Detroit: Macmillan, 2007.

Bermúdez Vázquez, Manuel. "Intuiciones De Criptojudaísmo En El "Quod Nihil Scitur" De Francisco Sánchez." Revista Internacional De Filosofía 13 (2008): 285-94.

Bermúdez Vázquez, Manuel. "La Influencia Del Pensamiento Judeo-cristiano En Michel De Montaigne, Giordano Bruno Y Francisco Sánchez." Ámbitos 23 (2010): 19-27.

Bodian, Miriam. "Hebrews of the Portuguese Nation: The Ambiguous Boundaries of Self-Definition." Jewish Social Studies 15, no. 1 (2008): 66-80.

Bodian, Miriam. Hebrews of the Portuguese Nation: Conversos and Community in Early Modern Amsterdam. Bloomington: Indiana University Press, 1997.

"B'nei Anusim." Be'chol Lashon. Accessed June 9, 2015. http://www.bechollashon.org/projects/spanish/anusim.php.

Carpenter, Dwayne. "From Al-Burak to Alboraycos: The Art of Transformation on the Eve of the Expulsion." In Jews and Conversos at the Time of the Expulsion. Jerusalem: Zalman Shazar for Jewish History, 1999.

Carvajal, Luis De, and Seymour B. Liebman. The Enlightened; the Writings of Luis De Carvajal, El Mozo. Coral Gables, Fla.: University of Miami Press, 1967.

Carvalho, Joaquim. Religion and Power in Europe: Conflict and Convergence. Pisa: PLUS-Pisa University Press, 2007.

Chazan, Robert. European Jewry and the First Crusade. Berkeley: University of California Press, 1987.

Cohen, Jeremy. "Between Martyrdom and Apostasy: Doubt and Self-definition in Twelfth-century Ashkenaz." Journal of Medieval and Early Modern Studies 29, no. 3 (1999): 431-71.

Cohen, Mark R. Under Crescent and Cross: The Jews in the Middle Ages. Princeton, N.J.: Princeton University Press, 1994.

Cohen, Shaye J. D. The Beginnings of Jewishness Boundaries, Varieties, Uncertainties. Berkeley: University of California Press, 1999.

"Conversos & Crypto-Jews." City of Albuquerque. Accessed June 9, 2015. http://www.cabq.gov/humanrights/public-information-and-education/diversity-booklets/jewish-american-heritage/conversos-crypto-jews.

"Crypto Jews." Am I Jewish? Accessed March 25, 2015. http://www.amijewish.info/w/crypto-jews/.

Cutler, Allan Harris, and Helen Elmquist Cutler. The Jew as Ally of the Muslim: Medieval Roots of Anti-Semitism. Notre Dame, Ind.: University of Notre Dame Press, 1986.

Davidson, Herbert A. Moses Maimonides: The Man and His Works. Oxford: Oxford University Press, 2005.

Dorff, Elliot N., and Arthur I. Rosett. A Living Tree the Roots and Growth of Jewish Law. Albany, N.Y.: State University of New York Press, 1988.

Faur, Jose. In the Shadow of History Jews and Conversos at the Dawn of Modernity. Albany, N.Y.: State University of New York Press, 1992.

Faur, José. "Four Classes of Conversos." Revue Des Études Juives 149, no. 1-2 (1990): 113-24.

Faur, José. "Anti-Maimonidean Demons." Review of Rabbinic Judaism 6 (2003): 3-52.

Ferry, Barbara, and Debbie Nathan. "Mistaken Identity? The Case of New Mexico's "Hidden Jews." The Atlantic. December 1, 2000. Accessed April 1, 2015. http://www.theatlantic.com/magazine/archive/2000/12/mistaken-identity-the-case-of-new-mexicos-hidden-jews/378454/ 1.

Ferziger, Adam S. "Between 'Ashkenazi' and Sepharad: An Early Modern German Rabbinic Response to Religious Pluralism in the Spanish-Portuguese Community." Studia Rosenthaliana 35, no. 1 (2001): 7-22.

Fishman, Talya. "The Jewishness of the Conversos." Lecture, Early Modern Workshop: Jewish History Resources, January 1, 2004.

Foer, Paul, and Chananette Pascal Cohen. "For Hispanic 'Crypto-Jews,' Lawsuits May Follow Religious Rediscovery." JNS. October 29, 2012. Accessed March 25, 2015. http://www.jns.org/latest-articles/2012/10/29/for-hispanic-crypto-jews-lawsuits-may-follow-religious-redis.html#.VXdW0dLBzGd.

Fram, Edward. "Perception and Reception of Repentant Apostates in Medieval Ashkenaz and Premodern Poland." AJS Review 21, no. 2 (1996): 299-339.

Frank, Daniel, and Matt Goldfish. Rabbinic Culture and Its Critics: Jewish Authority, Dissent, and Heresy in the Medieval and Early Modern Times. Detroit: Wayne State University, 2007.

Friedenwald, Harry. "Montaigne's Relation to Judaism and the Jews." The Jewish Quarterly Review 31, no. 2 (1940): 141-48.

Furst, Rachel. "Captivity, Conversion, and Communal Identity: Sexual Angst and Religious Crisis in Frankfurt, 1241." Jew History Jewish History 22, no. 1-2 (2008): 179-221.

Gampel, Benjamin R. "The 'Identity' of Sephardim of Medieval Christian Iberia." Jewish Social Studies 8, no. 2/3 (2002): 133-38.

Gerber, Jane S. The Jews of Spain. New York: The Free Press, 1992.

Gilman, Stephen. The Spain of Fernando De Rojas; the Intellectual and Social Landscape of La Celestina. Princeton, N.J.: Princeton University Press, 1972.

Gitlitz, David M. Secrecy and Deceit: The Religion of the Crypto-Jews. Philadelphia: Jewish Publication Society, 1996.

Goldish, Matt. The Sabbatean Prophets. Cambridge, Mass.: Harvard University Press, 2004.

Golinkin, David. "How Can Apostates Such as the Falash Mura Return to Judaism?" Responsa in a Moment 1, no. 5 (2007). Accessed June 9, 2015. http://www.schechter.edu/responsa.aspx?ID=30.

Gomez-Hortiguela Amillo, Angel. "La Vida Sine Querella De Juan Luis Vives." EHumanista 26 (2014): 345-56.

Grayzel, Solomon. "The Beginnings of Exclusion." The Jewish Quarterly Review 61, no. 1 (1970): 15-26.

Grayzel, Solomon. The Church and the Jews in the XIIIth Century. New York: Hermon, 1966.

Green, Simcha. "Welcoming Anusim Back Into The Family." The Jewish Press. August 22, 2012. Accessed March 25, 2015. http://www.jewishpress.com/indepth/opinions/welcoming-anusim-back-into-the-family/2010/12/08/0/?print.

Green, Toby. The Reign of Fear. London: Macmillan: 2007.

Guerson, Alexandra. "Seeking Remission: Jewish Conversion in the Crown of Aragon, C.1378–1391." Jewish History 24, no. 1 (2010): 33-52.

Gutwirth, Eleazar. "The Jews in 15th Century Castilian Chronicles." The Jewish Quarterly Review 74, no. 4 (1984): 379-96.

Halevy, Schulamith C., and Nachum Dershowitz. "Obscure Practices among New World Anusim." Proceedings of the Conferencia Internacional De Investigacion De La Asociacion Latinoamericana De Estudios Judaicos, 1995. Accessed June 9, 2015.

Haliczer, Stephen. "Conversos Y Judíos En Tiempos De La Expulsión : Un Análisis Crítico De Investigación Y Análisis." Revistas Espacio, Tiempo Y Forma Serie III (1993): 287-300.

"Jewish History Sourcebook: The Jews of Spain and the Visigothic Code, 654-681 CE." Fordham University. 1998. Accessed June 2, 2015. http://legacy.fordham.edu/halsall/jewish/jews-visigothic1.asp.

Halperin, David J. trans. Abraham Miguel Cardozo; Selected Writings. New York: Paulist Press, 2001.

Hayim Sofer, Yitshaq BenTsvi Ben Naftali. Sefer Shu " T Ha-Radbaz Mi-Ktav Yad. Benei Brak, 1975.

Hershman, A.M. Rabbi Isaac Bar Sheshet Perfet and His Times. New York, N.Y.: Jewish Theological Seminary, 1943.

Hinojosa Montalvo, José. "Los Judios En La España Medieval: De La Tolerancia a La Expulsión." In Los Marginados En El Mundo Medieval Y Moderno., 25-41. Almería: Instituto De Estudios Almerienses, 1998.

Hochbaum, Jerry. "Who Is a Jew: A Sociological Perspective." Tradition 13/14, no. 4/1 (1973): 35-41.

Hopstein, Avner. "The Crypto-Jews of Brazil." Y Net News. October 26, 2006. Accessed March 31, 2015. http://www.ynetnews.com/articles/0,7340,L-3319972,00.html.

Hordes, Stanley M. To the End of the Earth: A History of the Crypto-Jews of New Mexico. New York: Columbia University Press, 2005.

Idel, Moshe. Messianic Mystics. New Haven: Yale University Press, 1998.

Ingram, Kevin. Secret Lives, Public Lies the Conversos and Socio-religious Non-conformism in the Spanish Golden Age. San Diego, California: UC San Diego Electronic Theses and Dissertations, 2006.

Ingram, Kevin, ed. The Conversos and Moriscos in Late Medieval Spain and Beyond. Vol. 2. Leiden: Brill, 2012.

Israel, Jonathan. "Sephardic Immigration into the Dutch Republic, 1595-1672." Studia Rosenthaliana 23 (1989): 45-53.

Israel, Jonathan. "Spain and the Dutch Sephardim, 1609-1660." Studia Rosenthaliana 12, no. 1/2 (1978): 1-61.

Jacobs, Louis. "Attitudes towards Christianity in the Halakhah." Louis Jacobs. 2005. Accessed June 1, 2015. http://louisjacobs.org/articles/attitudes-towards-christianity-in-the-halakhah/?highlight=Attitudes towards Christianity.

Jocz, Jakob. The Jewish People and Jesus Christ; a Study in the Relationship between the Jewish People and Jesus Christ. London: S.P.C.K., 1949.

JOSPIC -J Staff "A List of 134 Books Containing Marrano, Converso, Crypto Jew, Secret Jew, Hidden Jew, New Christian, or Anusim in the Title or Subtitle: Changes in Usage Over 86 Years." Journal of Spanish, Portuguese, and Italian Crypto-Jews, 2011, 149-55.

Juster, J. Les Juifs Dans L'Empire Romain. Vol. II. Paris: P. Geunther, 1914.

Kaplan, Yosef. "The Portuguese Jews in Amsterdam: From Forced Conversion to a Return to Judaism." Studia Rosenthaliana 15, no. I (1981): 37-51.

Kaplan, Yosef. "The Jewish Profile of the Spanish-Portuguese Community of London during the Seventeenth Century." Judaism 41, no. 3 (1992): 229-40.

Kaplan, Yosef. "Wayward New Christians and Stubborn New Jews: The Shaping of a Jewish Identity." Jewish History 8, no. I-2 (1994): 27-41.

Katz, Jacob. Exclusiveness and Tolerance; Studies in Jewish-gentile Relations in Medieval and Modern Times. West Orange: Behrman House, 1961.

Katz, Jacob. Halakhah Ve-Qabbalah. Jerusalem: Magnes Press, 1984.

Katz, Solomon. The Jews in the Visigothic and Frankish Kingdoms of Spain and Gaul. New York: Kraus, 1970.

Kedourie, Elie. Spain and the Jews: The Sephardi Experience: 1492 and after. London: Thames and Hudson, 1992.

Kelly, David. "DNA Clears the Fog Over Latino Links to Judaism in New Mexico." Los Angeles Times. December 5, 2004. Accessed March 25, 2015. http://articles.latimes.com/2004/dec/05/nation/na-heritage5.

Kohut, George Alexander Jewish Martyrs of the Inquisition in South America New York: The Friedenwald Company, 1895.

Krow-Lucal, Martha G. "Marginalizing History: Observations on the Origins of the Inquisition in Fifteenth-century Spain by B. Netanyahu." Judaism, 1997, 47-62.

Kunin, David A. "Welcoming Back the Anusim: A Halakhic Teshuvah." Sephardim Hope. July 9, 2009. Accessed June 10, 2015. http://sephardimhope.net/index.php?view=article&catid=36:articles&id=62:welcoming-back-the-anusim-a-halakhic-teshuvah&format=pdf&option=com_content&Itemid=69.

Lavender, Abraham D. "The Secret Jews (Neofiti) of Sicily: Religious and Social Status Before and After the Inquisition." Journal of Spanish, Portuguese, and Italian Crypto-Jews 3 (2011): 119-33.

Lawrance, Jeremy. "Alegoría Y Apocalipsis En "El Alboraique"" Revista De Poética Medieval 11 (2003): 11-39.

Lazar, Moshe. The Jews of Spain and the Expulsion of 1492. Lancaster, Calif.: Labyrinthos, 1997.

Lea, Henry Charles. "Ferrand Martinez and the Massacres of 1391." The American Historical Review 1, no. 2 (1896): 209-19.

Leibman, Seymour. The Jews in New Spain. Miami: University of Miami, 1970.

Lent, Dani. "Analysis of the Israeli High Courts: Jewish Apostates and the Law of Return." Kol Hamevaser. 2010. Accessed June 1, 2015. http://www.kolhamevaser.com/2010/09/analysis-of-the-israeli-high-court-jewish-apostates-and-the-law-of-return/.

Lewis, Bernard. The Jews of Islam. Princeton, N.J.: Princeton University Press, 1984.

Lichenstein, Aharon. Brother Daniel and Jewish Fraternity, Leaves of Faith: The World of Jewish Living. Jersey City: Ktav, 2004.

Lieberman, Julia R. "Sermons and the Construct of a Jewish Identity: The Hamburg Sephardic Community in the 1620s." Jewish Studies Quarterly 10, no. 1 (2003): 49-72.

Liebman, Seymour B. The Jews in New Spain; Faith, Flame, and the Inquisition, Coral Gables, Fla.: University of Miami Press, 1970.

Liebman, Seymour B. New World Jewry, 1493-1825: Requiem for the Forgotten. New York: Ktav Pub. House, 1982.

Linder, Amnon. The Jews in Roman Imperial Legislation. Detroit, Mich.: Wayne State University Press, 1987.

Lindo, E.H. The Jews of Spain and Portugal. London: Longman, Brown, Green, & Longmans, 1848.

Lipshiz, Cnaan. "Secret No More." Shavei Israel. November 9, 2009. Accessed March 25, 2015. http://www.shavei.org/communities/bnei_anousim/articles-bnei_anousim/secret-no-more/?lang=en.

Llobet Portella, Josep Maria. "Los Conversos Según La Documentación Local De Cervera (1338-1501)." Revista De La Facultad De Geografia E Historia 4 (1989): 335-49.

Maimonides, Moses, and Abraham S. Halkin. Crisis and Leadership: Epistles of Maimonides. Philadelphia: Jewish Publication Society of America, 1985.

Marcus, Jacob Rader. The Jew in the Medieval World: A Source Book, 315-1791. Cincinnati: Union of American Hebrew Congregations, 1938.

Margaliot, Reuben. Sefer Ḥasidim. Jerusalem: Mosad Ha-Rav Ḳooḳ, 1956.

"Marranos, Conversos & New Christians." Jewish Virtual Library. Accessed June 1, 2015. https://www.jewishvirtuallibrary.org/jsource/Judaism/Marranos.html.

Martin, J. J. "Marranos and Nicodemites in Sixteenth-Century Venice." Journal of Medieval and Early Modern Studies 41, no. 3 (2011): 577-99.

Mentzer, Raymond A. "Marranos of Southern France in the Early Sixteenth Century." The Jewish Quarterly Review 72, no. 4 (1982): 303-11.

Metzger, David, ed. Sheelot U-Teshuvot Le-rabbenu Ha-gadol Marana Ve-rabbana Ha-rav Yizhak Bar Sheshet. Jerusalem: Makhon Or HaMizrah, 1993.

Meyers, Charles, and Norman Simms, eds. Troubled Souls: Conversos, Crypto-Jews, and Other Confused Jewish Intellectuals from the Fourteenth through the Eighteenth Century. Hamilton: Outrigger Publishers, 2001.

Meyerson, Mark D. "Aragonese and Catalan Jewish Converts at the Time of the Expulsion." Jewish History, 1992, 131-49.

Meyerson, Mark D. A Jewish Renaissance in Fifteenth-century Spain. Princeton: Princeton University Press, 2004.

Montalvo, Jose. The Jews of the Kingdom of Valencia: From Persecution to Expulsion, 1391-1492. Jerusalem: Magnes Press, Hebrew University, 1993.

Nelson, Zalman. "Is a Jew Who Converts Still Jewish?" Chabad. Accessed June 2, 2015. http://www.chabad.org/library/article_cdo/aid/1269075/jewish/Is-a-Jew-Who-Converts-Still-Jewish.htm.

Netanyahu, B. "Americo Castro and His View of the Origins of the Pureza De Sangre." Proceedings of the American Academy for Jewish Research 46/47, no. Jubilee Volume (1928-29 / 1978-79) (1979): 397-457.

Netanyahu, B. The Origins of the Inquisition in Fifteenth Century Spain. New York: Random House, 1995.

Netanyahu, B. The Marranos of Spain: From the Late 14th to the Early 16th Century, According to Contemporary Hebrew Sources. 3rd ed. Ithaca, N.Y.: Cornell University Press, 1999.

Nirenberg, David. "Conversion, Sex, And Segregation: Jews And Christians In Medieval Spain." The American Historical Review 107, no. 4 (2002): 1065-093.

Nirenberg, David. Anti-Judaism: The Western Tradition. New York: W. W. Norton &, 2013.

Nissimi, Hilda. "Religious Conversion, Covert Defiance and Social Identity: A Comparative View." Numen 51, no. 4 (2004): 367-406.

"Obituary Samuel Lerer, an American Rabbi Who Converted Mexicans, Dies at 89." Jewish Telegraph Agency. February 9, 2004. Accessed March 25, 2015. http://www.jta.org/2004/02/09/archive/obituary-samuel-lerer-an-american-rabbi-who-converted-mexicans-dies-at-89.

Oeltjen, Natalie. Crisis and Regeneration: The Conversos of Majorca, 1391-1416. Toronto: University of Toronto, 2012.

Orme, Wyatt. "Crypto-Jews' In the Southwest Find Faith in a Shrouded Legacy." Code Switch Frontiers of Race, Culture, and Ethnicity. February 19, 2014. Accessed March 25, 2015. http://www.npr.org/sections/codeswitch/2014/02/19/275862633/crypto-jews-in-the-southwest-find-faith-in-a-shrouded-legacy.

Parello, Vincent. "La Apologética Antijudía De Juan Luis Vives (1543)." Melanges De La Casa De Velazquez 38, no. 2 (2008): 171-87.

Perez, Joseph, and Lysa Hochroth. History of a Tragedy: The Expulsion of the Jews from Spain. Chicago: University of Illinois Press, 1993.

Perlmann, Moshe. "Apostasy." Jewish Virtual Library. 2008. Accessed June 2, 2015. http://www.jewishvirtuallibrary.org/jsource/judaica/ejud_0002_0002_0_01188.html.

Popkin, Richard H. The History of Scepticism from Erasmus to Spinoza. Rev. and Expanded ed. Berkeley: University of California Press, 1979.

"Portugal." Jewish Virtual Library, accessed on July 28, 2015, http://www.jewishvirtuallibrary.org/jsource/vjw/Portugal.html

Quesada Morillas, Yolanda. "La Expulsion De Los Judios Andaluces a Finales Del Siglo XV Y Su Prohibicion De Pase a Indias." Actas Del I Congreso Internacional Sobre Migraciones En Andalucia, 2011, 2099-106.

Rábade Obrado, María Del Pilar. "La Instrucción Cristiana De Los Conversos En La Castilla Del Siglo XV." En La España Medieval 22 (1999): 369-93.

Raphael, Amia. "Goldsmiths and Silversmiths." Jewish Virtual Library accessed on July 31, 2015. http://www.jewishvirtuallibrary.org/jsource/judaica/ejud_0002_0007_0_07579.html.

Rosenblatt, Eli. "Picturing Today's Conversos." The Forward. April 1, 2008. Accessed March 25, 2015. http://forward.com/culture/13079/picturing-today-s-conversos-01595/.

Rosenbloom, Noah H. "Menasseh Ben Israel and the Eternality of Punishment Issue." Proceedings of the American Academy for Jewish Research 60 (1994): 241-62.

Rosenstock, Bruce. "Abraham Miguel Cardoso's Messianism: A Reappraisal." AJS Review 23, no. 1 (1998): 63-104.

Ross, Theodore. "Shalom on the Range: In Search of the American Crypto-Jew." Harpers. December 1, 2009. Accessed March 27, 2015. http://harpers.org/archive/2009/12/shalom-on-the-range/.

Roth, Cecil. A History of the Marranos. Philadelphia: Jewish Publication Society of America, 1947.

Roth, Cecil. The Spanish Inquisition. New York: WW. Norton and Company, 1964.

Roth, Norman. "Anti-Converso Riots of the Fifteenth Century, Pulgar, and the Inquisition." En La España Medieval 15 (1992): 367-94.

Roth, Norman. Jews, Visigoths, and Muslims in Medieval Spain: Cooperation and Conflict. Leiden: E.J. Brill, 1994.

Roth, Norman. Conversos, Inquisition, and the Expulsion of the Jews from Spain. Madison, Wis.: University of Wisconsin Press, 1995.

Ruderman, David B. Jewish Thought and Scientific Discovery in Early Modern Europe. Detroit, Michigan: Wayne State University, 2001.

Sachar, Howard Morley. Farewell España: The World of the Sephardim Remembered. New York: Knopf, 1995.

Salomon, H.P. "New Light on the Portuguese Inquisition: The Second Reply to the Archbishop of Cranganor." Studia Rosenthaliana 5, no. 2 (1971): 178-86.

Sanchez, Francisco, and Douglas F.S. Thomson. That Nothing Is Known. Edited by Elaine Limbrick. Cambridge: Cambridge University Press, 1988.

Saperstein, Marc. "Christianity, Christians, and 'New Christians' in the Sermons of Saul Levi Morteira." Hebrew Union College Annual 70/71:329-84.

Saperstein, Marc. "Saul Levi Morteira's Treatise on the Immortality of the Soul." Studia Rosenthaliana 25, no. 2 (1991): 131-48.

Schiffman, Lawrence H. Who Was a Jew?: Rabbinic and Halakhic Perspectives on the Jewish-Christian Schism. Hoboken, N.J.: Ktav Pub. House, 1985.

Scholberg, Kenneth R. "Minorities in Medieval Castilian Literature." Hispania 37, no. 2 (1954): 203-09.

Scholem, Gershom. The Messianic Idea in Judaism: And Other Essays on Jewish Spirituality. New York: Schocken Books, 1972.

Selke, Angela. Los Chuetas Y La Inquicision. Madrid: Taurus, 1972.

Shatzmiller, Joseph. "Converts and Judaizers in the Early Fourteenth Century." Harvard Theological Review 74, no. 1 (1981): 63-77.

Sherwin, Byron L. Faith Finding Meaning: A Theology of Judaism. Oxford: Oxford University Press, 2009.

Singer, Isidore, and Cyrus Adler, eds. "Spain." Jewish Encylopedia. 1906.

Spinoza, Benedictus De, and Dagobert D. Runes. The Ethics Of Spinoza: The Road to Inner Freedom. Secaucus: Citadel, 1976.

Starr-LeBeau, Gretchen D. In the Shadow of the Virgin: Inquisitors, Friars, and Conversos in Guadalupe, Spain. Princeton, Princeton University Press, 2003.

Stern, Sacha. Jewish Identity in Early Rabbinic Writings. New York: Brill, 1994.

Stillman, Norman A. The Jews of Arab Lands: A History and Source Book. Philadelphia: Jewish Publication Society of America, 1979.

Suarez Bilbao, Fernando. "Cristianos Contra Judios y Conversos." Lecture, from Universidad Rey Juan Carlos, Madrid, January 1, 2004.

Swetschinski, Daniel M. "Kinship and Commerce: The Foundations of Portuguese Jewish Life in Seventeenth-Century Holland." Studia Rosenthaliana 15, no. I (1981): 52-74.

Synan, Edward A. The Popes and the Jews in the Middle Ages. New York: Macmillan, 1965.

Synan, Edward A. The Popes and the Jews in the Middle Ages. New York: Macmillan, 1965.

Szajkowski, Zosa. "Trade Relations of Marranos in France with the Iberian Peninsula in the Sixteenth and Seventeenth Centuries." The Jewish Quarterly Review 50, no. I (1959): 69-78.

Thornton, Stuart. "Hidden History: Rabbi Explains the Identity of the Crypto-Jews." National Geographic. Accessed March 25, 2015. http://www.nationalgeographic.com/hidden-history/.

Touger, Eliyahu. "Avodah Kochavim - Chapter Two." Chabad. Accessed June 9, 2015. http://www.chabad.org/library/article_cdo/aid/912360/jewish/Avodah-Kochavim-Chapter-Two.htm.

Touger, Eliyahu. "Ma'achalot Assurot - Chapter 17." Chabad. Accessed June 9, 2015.

http://www.chabad.org/library/article_cdo/aid/968273/jewish/Maachalot-Assurot-Chapter-17.htm.

Touger, Eliyahu. "Gerushin - Chapter Three." Chabad. Accessed June 9, 2015. http://www.chabad.org/library/article_cdo/aid/957708/jewish/Gerushin-Chapter-Three.htm.

Touger, Eliyahu. "Yibbum VChalitzah - Chapter One." Chabad. Accessed June 9, 2015. http://www.chabad.org/library/article_cdo/aid/960619/jewish/Yibbum-vChalitzah-Chapter-One.htm.

Treatman, Ronit. "Queen Esther: Patron Saint of Crypto-Jews." The Times of Israel. March 16, 2014. Accessed April 2, 2015. http://www.timesofisrael.com/queen-esther-patron-saint-of-crypto-jews/.

Usque, Samuel, and Martin Cohen. Consolations for the Tribulations of Israel (Consolacam as Tribulacoens De Israel). Philadelphia: Jewish Publication Society of America, 1977.

Utterback, Kristine T. ""Conversi" Revert: Voluntary and Forced Return to Judaism in the Early Fourteenth Century." Church History 64, no. 1 (1995): 16-28.

Wakefield, Walter L. Heresy, Crusade, and Inquisition in Southern France, 1100-1250. Berkeley: University of California Press, 1974.

Wheelwright, Jeff. "The 'Secret Jews' of San Luis Valley." Smithsonian Magazine. 2008. Accessed March 25, 2015. http://www.smithsonianmag.com/science-nature/the-secret-jews-of-san-luis-valley-11765512/?no-ist.

Wildman, Sarah. "Mallorca's Jews Get Their Due: Spanish Island's Community Alive and Thriving." The Forward. April 13, 2012. Accessed March 27, 2015. http://forward.com/articles/154649/mallorcas-jews-get-their-due/?p=all#ixzz3TLpkmfSl.

Wiznitzer, Arnold. "Crypto-Jews in Mexico during the Sixteenth Century." American Jewish Historical Quarterly 51, no. 3 (1962): 168-214.

Yerushalmi, Yosef. "The Re-education of the Marranos in the Seventeenth Century." Scribd. 1980. Accessed June 2, 2015. http://www.scribd.com/doc/63071643/Re-Education-of-the-Marranos-by-Yosef-Yerushalmi#scribd.

Yerushalmi, Yosef Hayim. "The Inquisition and the Jews of France in the Time' of Bernard Gui." Harvard Theological Review 63, no. 3 (1970): 317-76.

Yerushalmi, Yosef Hayim. From Spanish Court to Italian Ghetto; Isaac Cardoso; a Study in Seventeenth-century Marranism and Jewish Apologetics. New York: Columbia University Press, 1971.

Yovel, Yirmiyahu. "Converso Dualities In The First Generation: The Cancioneros." Jewish Social Studies: History, Culture, and Society 4, no. 3 (1998): 1-28.

Zeitlin, S. "Mumar and Meshumad." The Jewish Quarterly Review 54, no. 1 (1963): 84-86.

Zeldes, Nadia. "Legal Status of Jewish Converts to Christianity in Southern Italy and Provence." California Italian Studies, I, no. I (2010). Accessed June 2, 2015. http://escholarship.org/uc/item/91z342hv.

Zohar, Zvi. "The Sephardic Tradition-Creative Responses to Modernity." Lecture, January 1, 2010.

Zsom, Dora. "Uncircumcised Converts in Sephardi Responsa from the Fifteenth and Sixteenth Centuries." Iberoamerica Global 1, no. 3 (2008): 159-71.

Zsom, Dora. "The Return of the Conversos to Judaism in the Ottoman Empire and North-Africa." Hispania Judaica 7 (2010): 335-47.

Zsom, Dora. "Converts in the Responsa of R. David Ibn Avi Zimra: An Analysis of the Texts." Hispania Judaica 6 (2008): 267-92.

Zsom, Dora. "The Levirate Marriage of Converts in the Responsa of Some Sephardic Authorities." Kut 3 (2008): 96-113.

De Covarrubias Horozco, Sebastian. "Tesoro De La Lengua Castellana O Española." Universidad De Sevilla-Fondo Antiguo. Accessed June 2, 2015. http://fondosdigitales.us.es/fondos/libros/765/1119/tesoro-de-la-lengua-castellana-o-espanola/.

De Salazar Acha, Jaime. "La Limpieza De Sangre." Revista De La Inquisicion I (1991): 289-308.

De Spinoza, Benedict, and R.H.M Elwes. A Theologico-Political Treatise. New York: Dover, 1951.

.

Index

ABOUT THE AUTHOR

Juan Marcos Bejarano Gutierrez is a graduate of the University of Texas at Dallas where he earned a bachelor of science in electrical engineering. He works full time as an engineer but has devoted much of his time to Jewish studies. He studied at the Siegal College of Judaic Studies in Cleveland and received a Master of Arts Degree in Judaic Studies. He completed his doctoral studies at the Spertus Institute in Chicago in 2015. He studied at the American Seminary for Contemporary Judaism and received rabbinic ordination in 2011 from Yeshiva Mesilat Yesharim.

Juan Marcos Bejarano Gutierrez was a board member of the Society for Crypto-Judaic Studies from 2011-2013. He has published various articles in HaLapid, The Journal for Spanish, Portuguese, and Italian Crypto-Jews, and Apuntes-Theological Reflections from a Hispanic-Latino Context, and is the author of What is Kosher? and What is Jewish Prayer? and Secret Jews: The Complex Identity of Crypto-Jews and Crypto-Judaism. He is currently the director of the B'nai Anusim Center for Education at CryptoJewishEducation.com which provides additional information on the Inquisition as well as the phenomena of Crypto-Judaism.

If you have enjoyed this book or others that are part of this series, please consider leaving a positive review on Amazon or Goodreads. A positive review helps spread the word about this book and encourages others to study and learn something new.

87169856R00095

Made in the USA
San Bernardino, CA
02 September 2018